The God Principle

THE
GOD
PRINCIPLE

A Story of Amazing Connections
between Natural and Spiritual Realms

JOHN REKESH

ISBN-13: 978-0-9801516-7-1

Library of Congress Control Number: 2008901599

Published in the United States of America

Archress Literature:
Milpitas, CA 95035, USA.
http://www.archress.com

CONTENTS

1. INITIATION 13
The beginning.

2. DUST 19
Aliyah is given a hint on the spiritual meaning of the solar system.

3. DESERT 25
Aliyah discovers an important key to analyzing natural phenomena
and mapping those to spiritual phenomena.

4. STORM 35
Aliyah applies her newly found key to analyzing the systems of a storm.

5. CAR..47
Aliyah discovers that totally different realms could have common
principles behind them.

6. SKY 57
Aliyah finds a reflection of the mind and the search for enlightenment,
in the atmosphere that surrounds the earth.

7. RHYTHM 69
Aliyah maps the movement of the heavens to life on earth.

8. WEB 85
Aliyah recognizes various levels of evil, reflected in the habitat of a spider.

9. TREE OF LIFE 99
Aliyah connects with her higher self and finds its analogy in nature.

10. MOUNTAIN 113
Aliyah recognizes the past and the wondrous path ahead.

11. TREE OF KNOWLEDGE 125
Aliyah finds hints of deep connections between Darwinian and spiritual evolution.

12. PATH 137
Aliyah comes to understand physical and spiritual evolution as analogues of each other.

13. OVUM 149
Aliyah finds the origin of all creation reflected in an embryo.

14. SEA 157
Aliyah explores the human subconscious and its parallels in nature.

15. CHAOS 165
Aliyah explains the mission of Christ and more from natural laws.

16. WAR..177
Aliyah on war, the Mahabharata, and the forgiveness of sins.

17. EXODUS..197
Aliyah, the parting of the red sea, and the grand unification.

EPILOGUE..205

GLOSSARY 207

"To see a world in a grain of sand,
And a heaven in a wild flower,
Hold infinity in the palm of your hand,
And eternity in an hour."

William Blake

"All the truths of all the worlds are written all around us.
It only takes the eyes to see."

Anonymous

Foreword

There are books, and then there are books. *The God Principle* has a very special message to convey, perhaps bordering on the fantastical, yet absolutely real.

The primary message behind Aliyah's story is three-fold: The spiritual and the natural are *not* separate realms, they are one. They are even like *reflections* of each other. Secondly, there *is* meaning and purpose to life, which can be understood by carefully observing these natural-spiritual reflections. Finally, and perhaps most surprisingly, many conflicting viewpoints expressed by atheists, theists and agnostics can be seen as varying expressions of the *same truth*. In the pages that follow, it is hoped that the reader would find ample opportunity to pause, think, and consider the validity of this message.

Be warned that Aliyah covers territory from the mundane to the esoteric. The reader may find new concepts or connections in almost every chapter beyond the first, requiring active thought. Often it demands a focused attention, as concepts take the center stage, rather than the story line. Indeed, the terms *'mundane'* and *'esoteric'* are but relative terms. Perhaps the reader will discover that to understand one is to understand the other!

A glossary is provided at the end, covering certain concepts and terms used in the book.

Now on to Aliyah's story!

1. Initiation

The beginning.

S he ran out and into the woods, her hair flowing wildly, tears streaming down her cheeks, sobbing, arms flailing as her legs sought to carry her to the solace of her favorite abode in the heart of the woods.

And as she ran she wept, "Mother, oh, Mother, where are you? Why do you not help me? Do you not see that I am loveless and forsaken? How could you leave me and go away? Mother, where are you? What have I done to deserve this?"

She shouted as she ran and then threw herself down onto the grass, her body wrenched with sobs. There she lay, in a collapsed bundle, unable to think anymore, as she felt the very agony of being coursing through her. A long wail arose, which became a moan that persisted until it was swamped out by the wind.

Time and again she called out, "Mother! Mother! Where are you?" The silence in between her wails was broken only by the quiet, rustling sound of the wind as it swept through the grass and the cry of a lark somewhere close. Her body shook and shivered as she gave in to the very depth of her emotions, and the hurt within flowed out freely in abandon. And there arose in her a simple, but deep, burning question: "Why?" It seemed to come forth and explode within, as she gave way to the deepest existential sorrow that she had ever experienced.

As she lay in that sunlit clearing in the woods, a hush seemed to come over the land. It was as if the whole universe paused to listen to her plaintive cry, for what came from her soul was something much deeper.

She arose, turned her face towards the heavens, and shouted as she addressed the powers that be: "Why me? Who am I? What am I doing here? Can you hear me?"

Out poured a barrage of accusations and questions from her very being, as if she sought to elicit some kind of a response or help from the heavens. She desperately hoped for a miracle, that something would happen and she would be free of her misery. But no angel appeared to comfort her, nor did any voice speak to answer her troubles. No one came searching for her and nobody seemed to even care that she existed, so complete was her feeling of desolation.

The light started to fade and thunder clapped in the distance. Standing knee deep in the grass, staring up and screaming something incomprehensible, her hair and dress flowing in the wind, she appeared a wild and strange figure to the first drops of rain that descended from the heavens. And the rain poured down incessantly, painting the landscape gray as drop after drop landed in a steady stream on her face, mingling with her tears. The wind grew stronger and beat against her body, threatening to push her down into the grass.

She refused to budge, and set her face against the sky, a deep determination stealing into her being.

"I will not let you go without an answer," she screamed, as she pointed an accusing finger right into the heavens. "I am like the grass of the earth, trodden underfoot and crushed by everything that goes by. My roots are small, and I am but little, but I am no less determined than this grass at my feet. You have no wind strong enough to break me. No matter what you do to me, I shall rise up again and again and again, until you are forced to acknowledge me and give me what I seek. You cannot crush me forever, mow me down, burn me in fire or spoil me in desolation, for I shall rise again and demand of you my justice. What I do is right in my sight, and nothing you can tell me will ever convince me otherwise."

Shouts, accusations, frustration and fury followed one another as she poured them out into the universe and to her God, as her emotions churned into a single timeless moment of outrage. Her voice seemed to rise high above the rain, wind and the thunder, as it sought the highest heavens, looking for someone or something to smother in turn with its own burst of thunder.

But the very next moment, the futility of her outburst struck her so hard that she dropped her chin and collapsed once more to the ground, a sobbing, whimpering bundle in the grass. And there she lay, for a long time, eyes closed, the spasms in her body becoming ever more infrequent as they melted away into a gentle silence. The rain too stopped pouring, becoming a drizzle that soon thinned out further and disappeared. And there she lay for a very long time.

The sunlight was again streaming through the clearing as she sat up and looked around. Something had changed. She felt a calm stillness within as she surveyed her surroundings. Everything around her seemed somehow more alive than before. Perhaps the colors were more vibrant, the textures sharper, the smell of the woods stronger, the cry of the lark sweeter, for it seemed that every feature of the landscape seemed to vie for her attention.

She did not analyze it, but simply sat there, still drenched, as a gentle, comforting solace seeped in from all around. It was as though Mother Nature were holding her in her bosom, and comforting her through her sorrow. She basked in that rarely felt solace, all thought of sorrow at bay, and she breathed in life and breathed out her worries. She felt a strange kinship, a kind of compassion within, as she looked at the grass she had identified with in her outburst.

"We are a lot like each other," she told the grass, and was surprised at the new clarity with which she could observe it. The blades all seemed to stand out, each like an individual, as they all grew in profusion in various paths, and bent and moved in the wind. The shoots that grew forth and held seed pods or flowers looked like giant trees against the blue sky. The soil looked like a vast terrain, little pebbles like big rocks, rivulets of water like rivers, as the grass suddenly became a forest, vibrant and alive, teeming with life. Drops of water on the grass echoed the sun a million-fold, like an all-embracing cosmic presence. And they all seemed to want to say something, *as if they had many a story to tell.*

But other than the strange wonder that filled her, there was nothing she could understand from what she observed and felt, except for a curious sense of deep connection with all around her. They evoked a response in her heart, and tears came as she looked around. Not only, she felt, was the grass like her, but also the rocks, the trees, the lark and even the sky. Her sense of compassion extended itself to everything around her, and she identified with it and tried to experience the world as it did. Everything around seemed a reflection of herself, innocent, trusting, having no purpose, no plan and direction, having no choice – but just being what they were, singing their song.

It was again a long time before she stood up and walked back home. The sun was setting, and she was no further from her confusion than before, but inwardly there was a peculiar contentment. The day had evoked a strange magic in her heart, creating a deepened sense of connection with nature.

That day she had found the Mother she had missed so much in her life. From now on Mother Earth would be her mother always. In her she was to find comfort, solace, and soon, instruction. Time and again she was to rush back to her mother whenever things seemed to go wrong, events took a depressing turn, and life seemed to impose such a heavy burden that nothing seemed to offer any meaning or purpose. Her great escape was into the bosom of her Mother, where she sought to understand and make sense of what happened around her. It would be still many years before she found her Father, and many more before she found herself. For the path from motherly love and fatherly correction to a flowering maturity is a long, arduous path and there was much she was yet to discover and learn in the hands of time, as it seemed to stretch, draw out, spin and weave into a tapestry, the very essence of her being.

It was to be a long journey into herself.

2. Dust

Aliyah is given a hint on the spiritual meaning of the solar system.

The dust drifted and swirled around, forming currents and eddies as she watched. It was huge, beyond description. Each one of its grains seemed alive, moving of its own volition, yet yielding to the greater swirls and eddies within a great movement that seemed to stretch from infinity to infinity. She felt she could sense subtle emotions, thoughts and aspirations within those currents of dust, as though they yearned to seek expression. They moved about in strange patterns, swirling, merging, separating, even chasing one another. Something within them was laboring hard to come forth and manifest. The Great Void now looked alive, seething with activity, harboring the tiniest to the largest forms in its womb.

As she watched, the patterns of dust took on denser forms as they dragged in more and more dust, till an uncountable multitude of patterns were stretched across the vastness of space. They undulated and moved against one another and then started coalescing, at first slowly, then faster and faster, until a huge whirlpool formed in their midst. The entire body of dust was now shrinking rapidly, twisting and dragged in by the force of the whirlpool, and pattern after pattern disappeared into its depths. It looked as though the Great Void had taken a deep breath, dragging all its aspirations into itself.

Time stood still, and nothing existed anytime or anywhere. Just when she thought everything was gone for good, a bright light appeared where the whirlpool had been. The light expanded, growing faster and brighter, till it gave way to a tremendous explosion. It seemed that the Great Void was now breathing out all its aspirations and patterns into an explosive form that scattered all over space, and right through her.

Time seemed to fly now, and she looked on, fascinated, for the light threw itself far and wide into forms of swirling masses and colors strewn across space. There was a great light where the whirlpool had been, a tremendous powerhouse from which streamed forth endless light and energy that bathed the Great Void with its luminescence. The Great Light appeared almost alive. Those masses swirling around in space had coalesced into solid-looking spheres as they moved around their Creator. She thought another whirlpool might form now, but some unknown force held them to their paths. It seemed that the great central light was exerting its will on them, ordering their paths, yet allowing them to develop in their own way. Each one of them looked like different universes unto themselves, some having galaxies. They all had condensed into very different forms from the same essence of their creator. And they moved around their creator, as if paying homage, in an endless circle of worship.

'Aliyah,' came a soft and gentle voice, hardly audible. Someone was calling her. She strained and listened. The voice came again, this time more clearly. It was a melodious voice, gentle and full of love. She looked about her, trying to ascertain where the voice had come from. It sounded as if one of those ethereal forms of universes moving in the Great Void was actually calling to her. She moved closer to study them and the voice became more audible. The next moment, she found herself staring at a great, luminous orb clothed in blue and white against the backdrop of the great light. She knew she was looking at the Earth. She could see its beautiful blue oceans, the emerald green forests, the continents and dusty-brown deserts, and the shiny white masses of clouds that wrapped around it like garlands. The voice called her name again gently. And as she looked, there was movement on the Earth. The oceans, forests, continents and the clouds moved around slowly, forming shapes and figures both familiar and unfamiliar, and soon she was staring at a beautiful face that appeared in their midst.

"Mother?" she called out, her heart beating fast, for this was the face of her own mother, long lost to time, whom she remembered only from photographs. To see her now was a shock, and she drew in her breath sharply. The face broke into a beautiful smile and she felt she had never seen anything so beautiful in her whole life. She rushed forward as a great emotion overwhelmed her and she found herself falling headlong towards the Earth, towards the face of her mother etched into the clouds, oceans and the continents. But as soon as she started falling, the pattern began to change, as the masses started shifting again. They seemed to be moving in rhythm with her fall, and the beautiful smile was now twisted into a painful and ugly howl, and the face changed from the angelic beauty that it once was into a demonic countenance of utter and diabolical evil. Its visage filled her with horror and revulsion. She screamed as she hit the atmosphere like a flaming meteor, rushing helplessly towards the evil form stretched out below, as it dragged her to itself.

She woke up screaming. This was not the first time that her dreams, which started gently and beautifully, had turned into a nightmare. Panting and sweating profusely, she tried to calm her nerves and assure herself that everything was all right. It was dawn and the first light was coming in through the drapes of her windows.

The light was a welcome sight and it so quickly allayed her fears that she started breathing normally, emotions in control. Her deeply analytical mind took over and tried to make sense of the dream. Of course it must have been that book on astronomy she was reading before going to bed. What she saw in the dream was probably a rendition of the origin of the solar system, though there were some strange elements that came into the dream that gave it a mystical twist. Her yearning for motherly love and her love of nature must have colored the latter part of the dream.

At age twenty one, she was almost an atheist. Life had been quite hard until now. Orphaned at an early age, her father having died in the war, and her mother during childbirth, she had struggled through housework and school, living with a relative who took her in. But there was a deep passion in her, something that carried her through life's many setbacks. And setbacks there were, indeed, for she was subject to ridicule and neglect, cruelty and abuse, and she fell asleep many a night with eyes swollen and tears still drying on her cheeks. But through persistence and hard work, she had won a scholarship for college. And now life held true promise.

Throughout all those years, she had developed a deep grudge against God. This came from her own feeling of desolation, her observation of human suffering, and her study of nature, all of which portrayed a life often "red in tooth and claw." Her analytical mind had decided that no God could create or permit such a life and therefore He could not exist. Yet she was curious about other modes of thought, of various religions and philosophies. And she studied them to find out what made them tick.

For that reason, her dream was particularly striking, as many aspects of it kept coming back to her mind. She recognized that it held a dazzling portrayal of the solar system as an analogue of something else. A great void with subtle aspirations, a powerful creator, manifested universes and their relationships all seemed to be portrayed through a simple analogy of dust and the solar system. She had in the past come across philosophies that discussed a Void as the source of everything, and from which was somehow birthed a creator who was responsible for many universes. It was as though a concept discussed endlessly in some philosophical circles had a natural rendition for anyone who cared to look and see.

Quickly her analytical mind asserted itself. "Look Aliyah," it said. "You *know* that this was just a crazy dream. What you saw about the origin of the solar system was just a cloud of dust and the birth of a star. What was that part about your mother and a daemon? It was downright silly. All this is just a jumble thrown up by your subconscious, a projection of your futile yearning for meaning and purpose. You know there is no creator, let alone a God. Hasn't life proved that to you yet? So why are you taken in by these wild ideas?"

She forcefully pushed her thoughts aside and got up from bed. Today was going to be exciting, she thought, a weekend escape to one of her most favorite places. She had better hurry, for she knew better than to keep Emma waiting.

It was a new day, and a new beginning.

3. Desert

Aliyah discovers an important key to analyzing natural phenomena and mapping those to spiritual phenomena.

Treks into the rocky desert were always something to look forward to. She had a strange fascination with that terrain, for she found it indescribably beautiful and never missed an opportunity to spend some hours alone with the desert.

"Here I am, driving a hundred miles through godforsaken country just so that you can stare at a ghastly skeleton in the middle of nowhere," Emma grumbled as she threw up her hands in mock frustration. "This is the last time, hon. I am not going to indulge you anymore."

Emma was her good friend, though quite her opposite in nature. A gregarious party animal and always ready for a bit of fun, for Emma, excitement in life meant clothes, people, parties and cars. She found Aliyah a strange girl, quite unlike herself, and she couldn't figure out what brought them close. Still Emma enjoyed talking to Aliyah and listening to her wild and crazy ideas. They always made her pause, and think again.

Emma parked her Beetle in the shade of a big rock and watched Aliyah clamber out into the sunshine.

"Not me, hon," she said, "It gives me the creeps. Besides, I have a lot of catch up to do with my reading."

With the air conditioning and stereo on full blast, Emma pulled out a novel, some popcorn and soda cans, pulled back her seat and was soon transported into a much more exciting world than the forlorn desert she left behind.

Aliyah took a deep breath. The desert was as inviting as always: the hot winds, azure blue sky, visibility from horizon to horizon, sandstone rocks sculpted by winds into other-worldly forms, small shrubs and cacti for greenery, an occasional movement as a lizard crawled hurriedly beneath a rock. Here was nature in raw and stark splendor. It looked practically lifeless to the casual observer, but she knew it was just an appearance. Even in such extreme conditions, life thrived, almost hidden. A lot of it existed as raw potential in the ground, and all it took was a brief spell of rain to transform the desert into a fleeting paradise of grass, shrubs and carpets of exquisite flowers, replete with insects and small animals. The rains would visit the desert rarely and briefly, and the quick but evanescent transformations she had seen then had been nothing short of miraculous.

And indeed, this was reminiscent of her own social work with deprived children, for she had found that their lives were arid and dry like this desert and a shower of love was what they needed to bring forth their potential to flower and fruit. For this reason she had long associated water and rain with love. The sparkling clear water that fell as rain from the skies she associated with a heavenly love, and her own tears for the children she associated with an earthly love.

And this love could transform lives, as she had seen. To her, many human lives were also like deserts, seeking expression, hoping for a miracle of rain to rejuvenate them, and yet none seemed to be forthcoming. An occasional shower brought in a period of tremendous activity and fulfillment, and then life went back to a normal, apparently lifeless routine. Here was a reflection of her own life, and perhaps that of millions of others. The earth teemed with many lush ecosystems, but nearly one-tenth of its human population somehow chose to, or were forced to, live in desert lands. She found a tremendous symbolism there.

Was it that the desert represented some sort of purgatory? In allegories, it stood for trials and tribulations, and it was a curious fact that many of the world's great religions and spiritual traditions arose in arid or desert lands. The sandy deserts such as in the Middle East, the arid plains and plateaus such as those in India, and the cold and rocky deserts found in Tibet or China were ample testimony to this. She knew that dusts from the deserts were carried up daily into the sky by winds, and across continents, where they served as the condensation nuclei for clouds and water drops. And they came down as showers of rain, at the center of every life-giving drop. So had the spiritual teachings, traditions and their messengers that lived through scorching tribulations and the purgatory of a desert-like life, traveled far from their homelands, guided by invisible forces, and sought to bring down a shower of heavenly love and life to nations and cultures around the world. The desert was a perfect allegory of a life being prepared in spiritual development. Didn't Jesus go into the desert to be tempted by the devil prior to His ministry? And wasn't it true that the sweetest fruit and the juiciest fruit grew in the desert? [1]

She found it very curious that such landscapes existed on the earth, when two-thirds of the planet was covered with

---

[1] Dates and watermelons respectively. Dates have more than 66% sugar content, as per USDA Agricultural Research Service Nutrient Data Lab.

oceans and water was being cycled through the atmosphere. She knew that some deserts faced the oceans, and some existed in proximity to forests. Such apparent barrenness in proximity to abundant life was quite a surprise. Yet they came about naturally through the action of the elements, and so did other ecosystems like the grasslands, the forests and so on. It looked like a whole spectrum of living conditions, from purgatory to paradise naturally co-existed in the same universe.

The wind kicked up dust in her face and she covered her eyes for a moment. When she looked again, a small vortex of moving air, like a miniature tornado, was stealing through the ground, rising up a cloud of dust that moved with it. The dust rose because there was little moisture in the ground and therefore no shrubs or grasses to hold it in place. The same winds had sculpted curious shapes out of the rocks. The action of wind, water and heat had caused the inexorable weathering of the body of earth, breaking cliffs into boulders and boulders into smaller rugged stones, even dust. These elements were so powerful that they had caused whole mountain ranges to disappear over eons.

Indeed, the ancients had always held that everything was composed of the elements they called earth, wind, water and fire. Quite understandable, she reflected, given their lack of scientific understanding. But how could they really describe anything, using that system, let alone a complex human being with body, mind and emotions? Or perhaps they could be allegories? Maybe it was indeed possible to describe a human being with that system?

This was a curious thought. The body was obviously formed from the elements of the earth, and she did associate water with love, or emotions. Its frozen form, ice, was often associated with a lack of emotion. And air, or breath, to the animal body was like the mind to human civilization – animating it, giving it life. And mind, like the air, was intangible and invisible. Air currents could then be an allegory to thoughts. The atmosphere of air around the planet was layered much like an onion, and she had a similar concept of the mind as well. Perhaps fire was an allegory for the so-called spirit. This was a curious association. Did the four elements of earth, wind, water and fire correspond to the realms of body, mind, emotions and spirit?

She sat down upon a rock and faced the setting sun, her hair flowing in the wind. There was a poetic beauty in everything that surrounded her, something that resonated deeply within her soul. But why? she asked herself. Why do I find the desert so beautiful and appealing? Is it that this terrain carries some deep reflection of myself? Does what happen here have anything to do with my own nature? The thought refused to go away and she considered it further.

Indeed, all the terrains of the earth, like the deserts, forests, grasslands and others, were created by the interplay of the elements of earth, wind, water and heat. And so were the storms, the lightning, clouds, rain, and in fact, everything she could observe. *Does a similar interplay in the realms of body, mind, emotions and spirit create similar phenomena?* If the allegory with the four elements were true, then this had to be so! Was it possible that these stones, dust, heat and the few clouds above are parallels or allegories of things that happen within human beings? Would it mean that all the ecosystems of the earth had corresponding allegories in human lives?

This was an exciting thought to her. Her musings on the sandy desert and rains did correspond to a spiritual message from the desert. Then thinking about rains, the phenomenon of acid rain came to mind. The acidity in the water, she knew, was due to pollutants in the air. As the air element seemed to represent the mind, by analogy the pollution of the air pointed out a corresponding pollution of the human mind. And the rain that fell through the air picked up the pollutants, pointing to a parallel corruption of emotions that resulted in corrosive and destructive behavior, much like acid. The pollutants, she observed, mostly came from the burning of fossil fuels, like petroleum and coal mined from the bowels of the earth. These fuels, both solid and liquid, corresponded to her basic instincts or bodily drives, the physical and emotional cravings, originating deep within her own animal nature. Or did they?

The coal taken deep from the bowels of the earth, by analogy, corresponded to physical drives of the body, its genetic inheritance of aggression and sexuality that generated so much power. Petroleum pointed to deep-seated and flammable emotions that also originated from within the body. Indeed, the fossil fuels were the solid and liquefied remains of organisms taken from the depths of the earth, representing natures that originated deep within the physical body. And these fuels had tremendous energy in them, just as there existed tremendous compulsions arising from basic instincts. These fuels had to be burnt to release their energy, the burning representing the fire element. This corresponded to the spirit that indulged in these experiences, with each instance of indulgence leaving its mark in the mind, polluting it further, and creating corrosive emotions. Likewise, the fossil fuels burned and polluted the air and turned rain acidic. Indeed, human civilization at large was driven by these fossil fuels, and likewise most human beings were also driven by their basic instincts. The allegories seemed valid, and she felt she had stumbled onto something. Perhaps there was a real connection between the earth-wind-water-fire system and body-mind-emotion-spirit system!

Could she combine the acid rain phenomenon with the allegory of the spiritual message from the desert? It seemed she could. The human mind had twisted even those life-giving spiritual showers into deadly ones, and she needed to look no further than the activities of destructive religious bigots and terrorists to find their echoes in the acid rain. The allegories still appeared valid.

What about the destructive storms, the tornadoes, the tsunamis and other phenomena that wreak havoc on the earth? She thought these too might have their analogies in human lives, for they too were actions of water, wind and heat on the earth. The strong winds and the huge waves were representative of a turbulent and violent mind giving way to emotional outbursts and physical destruction. Such natures existed within her, and in fact within everyone, from the scale of individuals to groups and even to nations. And their outcomes were as destructive as the storms, tornadoes or tsunamis. Once again, the association rang true.

But wasn't it just a coincidence, she wondered, or simply poetic imagination? Do the various phenomena in the realm of earth, wind, water and fire really reflect those in the realm of body, mind, emotions and spirit? What was spirit anyway? She was aware of religious and spiritual lore about various myths of hells and heavens, realms of the so-called spirit. If the fire-spirit analogy were true, then it meant that various patterns created on the earth by the elements reflected patterns from the so-called hells to the highest heavens! Indeed, her comparison of the desert to a religious purgatory did fall in line with this notion.

"Beware of the skeleton!" came an eerie voice from behind. Aliyah jumped and almost fell down. She turned around to find Emma doubled up in laughter.

"You really scared me there for a moment!" Aliyah exclaimed.

Emma was referring to the old sun-bleached remains of a steer, which seemed to fascinate Aliyah so much that she made a point of visiting it every time she arrived here.

"Here, dab some of this on yourself." Emma held out a bottle of suntan lotion. "And damn this heat! I hope it's doing my complexion some good. I'm already half-cooked."

Aliyah laughed as she took the proffered bottle. She was touched by her friend's concern.

"Well, I hope we don't get stranded in this place. My shoes are not made for walking," Emma tried again.

"You could leave them here for Prince Peter. I'm sure he will come to your rescue!" replied Aliyah, referring to Emma's boyfriend, who had a persistent habit of keeping tabs on her.

Emma smiled and looked around.

"If only he knew where we were! But cell phones are no use here. I'm afraid we may not have enough beetle juice to get us all the way back home."

Beetle juice was Emma's term for gasoline.

"Well, it's only a hundred miles of rocks, cacti and poisonous critters. I'm sure we can leg it."

Emma laughed and looked at Aliyah curiously. Trying to scare her was fun. But there was something else going on.

"What were you so engrossed in that you didn't hear me coming? That skeleton told you something new today?"

"No, Emma," Aliyah poured out to her friend. "But I think I found another skeleton, a live one that holds worlds in its sinews. Do you know what it means to see a world in a grain of sand?"

"The world? In a grain of sand?" laughed Emma. "I read that in some poetry lessons in high school. It's stuff for dreaming minds, pretty daft, if you ask me."

But then Emma paused and reflected on what Aliyah had said. She knew Aliyah was not kidding, and perhaps there was something in it, after all.

"Well, tell me all about it, hon, but not now," Emma continued, "The weather seems to be turning for the worse. We'd better get out of here."

Aliyah looked towards the western horizon. Indeed, the light was fading and clouds were gathering in the evening sky. It seemed that the desert was finally being visited by rain! Aliyah turned around, excited. She really wanted to stay back, but then saw Emma's disapproving look, and sighed.

"Going back so soon! I wish we could have stayed longer!"

"Yeah, and grow roots like a cactus! You hardly move from where you sit. If prairie dogs were really dogs, you would be all wet by now."

They both laughed. Aliyah promised herself to be back again soon, for this was something she did not want to miss – the wonderful and incomparable transformation of a desert! For now, they had to leave.

They walked back to the Beetle and got inside. Emma gave a sigh of relief when the car started without a hitch.

"Whew!" she said, "I was kind of scared that she may not start. Like in those movies you know? Get stranded here and ..."

"Come on, you worry wart! What could possibly happen?"

"Well, for me, it could be getting stuck in the middle of this desert. For you, it could be running into Prince Charming!" Emma took a jibe at Aliyah's inherent distrust of men that had kept her away from a serious relationship. Emma had really tried some matchmaking in the past, with little success.

"Well, don't look at me! Your princes have always turned into frogs, sooner or later."

Emma laughed, and then sighed. She had really hoped that Aliyah would pull out of all this nonsense if she were to get herself into a serious relationship. So far, that had not materialized.

"Just keep your eyes on the road, and we'll be fine." Aliyah admonished her.

The car pulled out from the shade of the big rock, soon entered the lone desert road, and headed west.

"Yeah, what could possibly happen?" Emma repeated to herself.

4. Storm

Aliyah applies her newly found key to analyzing the systems of a storm.

The car sped ahead and Emma listened to what Aliyah had to say about her discovery in the desert. She seemed to say that a consistent reflection of human lives was painted all around them in various phenomena, and that they could be analyzed by a simple system of correspondences: that the earth-wind-water-fire system was an analogy for the body-mind-emotion-spirit system.

'Hon, that's all very well, but it stretches my imagination too much. Perhaps there is some truth about the blasted weather, but anyone can take anything and then associate it with something else, find some common ground. Poets and dreamers do it all the time," Emma countered.

"That's true, Emma. But do you think that such common ground exists because there might be some deep relationships there? Poets might be recognizing them intuitively. Newton is said to have discovered the law of gravitation when he saw a falling apple. So there is valid common ground between a falling apple and the earth moving around the sun, or for that matter, with the tides or even day and night."

"Well, that's scientific stuff. But what you are saying is hardly so. I mean, why should there be any connection between the air and the mind at all? That's silly, if not atrocious!"

"I know what you mean. But any theory rests on unproven postulates. As long as conclusions from a theory are consistent, meaning they don't contradict one another, and they can explain as well as predict, then that theory must be given due consideration."

"So what does your newfangled notion explain or predict? The postulates are practically preposterous." Emma laughed at her own alliteration.

Aliyah sighed. "You raise a valid point, Emma. I just don't know. From what I see there seems to be some sort of connection. I only wonder what it could be."

Darkness fell rapidly and Emma turned on the car's headlights. A flash of lightning suddenly lit up the sky, followed by a deep clap of thunder. The sky was soon dark with storm clouds. Emma shivered.

"Nice day for an outing. I hate thunderstorms," she grimaced. "Why did you have to pick this day for a trip? We could be struck by lightning or get blown over by the wind. I can feel it; the wind is really getting strong. I should've checked the weather report before we started."

Within moments, the rain pattered down, soon turning into a downpour. With the wipers on at full blast, Emma peered ahead, trying to keep the car steady and on the road. The sky lit up again and again with flashes of light, followed by deafening roars of thunder.

"Now tell me what this storm means, if you can," yelled Emma over all the commotion in the air. She appeared a little frightened.

"Well, it does sound a little like you, doesn't it?" Aliyah teased as she gazed up into the sky through the window. Lightning seemed to be flashing inside the clouds, and between them, lighting up the sky. And once in a while, a bolt of lightning speared down from the sky and hit the earth. Another natural phenomenon from the elements. What does it correspond to in our lives?, she wondered as she mulled it over.

Lightning was a release of electrical energy between oppositely charged areas of a cloud or between clouds. And often it involved the ground as well. Oppositely charged clouds! Clouds were large aggregations of water drops and ice crystals condensed around minute particles of dust. The body-emotions analogy was obvious in the dust-water system of a thundercloud. Clouds, then, corresponded to the emotional natures of individuals, groups of people, or even nations. Oppositely charged clouds or areas of a cloud pointed to emotional polarities between groups, or even within a single individual.

And the role of ice was particularly striking, for it was the ice, the frozen form of water, that primarily caused the charge buildup in the clouds through friction, setting up polarities. Likewise it was the coldness or freezing of noble emotions, and rubbing one another the wrong way that created emotional charges between people. Then lightning occurred, a release of the pent-up charge. Likewise, the pent-up emotional charge in human beings was often released between people in conflict and aggression, even war.

And just as the lightning also hit the earth and destroyed what it touched, so did the conflict between human beings spew destruction on mother earth. The lightning heated up its path in the air to an extreme temperature, causing an explosion of hot air perceived as thunder. This reminded Aliyah of verbal assaults and war cries, the booming of cannons, the roars of missiles and the massive explosions of bombs accompanied by flashes of light as they released their destructive energy. The turbulent thunderclouds even held an analogy of mankind at war with itself!

"Really?" Emma now questioned, listening to Aliyah's description of a thundercloud. "So what makes them different from a normal cloud?"

"What is a normal cloud? There are many kinds, but I guess you are referring to all that are not thunderclouds. Well, there are the cirrus clouds, stratus clouds and many others, each having their own peculiarities."

"And how are they different?"

"The main difference seems to be that they are not overloaded with ice and water, and do not generate the huge amounts of static electricity charges that a thundercloud generates. So obviously they correspond to the gentle and nobler side of our emotions. And they do appear white, don't they? Like angels arrayed in white, high up in the sky…whereas the thunderclouds with their anvils look dark and dangerous. I guess the analogy is obvious. But the interesting point is that this correspondence seems to be not just in appearances, but also in the internal systems, the mechanisms that make the clouds behave as they do."

Emma fell silent. It seemed that Aliyah had a point there. She would have expected a peripheral similarity between thunderclouds and human nature, but it seemed that the analogy went a little deeper, into the systems that formed thunderclouds.

"So what about all this wind and rain? There's even hail falling down on us. How could that relate to thunderclouds, or to us?"

"Emma, this whole storm, including the clouds, lightning, wind and rain, is but a single system. What you see as a thundercloud up there is only the visible part of this system. Imagine that huge streams of warm, moist air are rising upwards and into the thundercloud, whereas cold air streams are coming down. There is a huge air circulation within the cloud. The two opposing factions of hot and cold moisture-laden winds blow into each other and create all kinds of phenomena, including storms, tornadoes, lightning, hail, and so on. You might compare these to a warfront where armies with opposing ideals and emotions meet and fight."

"Hmm... why do you say that?"

"Well, the strong moisture-laden winds correspond to emotionally charged thoughts that make us aggressive. These are the ones that are capable of wreaking all kinds of havoc. So you can see that the internal systems of the storm do seem to carry some reflection of our emotional natures."

Emma said nothing and pondered what Aliyah had said. Then she found a problem.

"But thunderclouds nourish us; they bring us rain," she objected.

"Yes, you're right." Aliyah paused for a moment, then continued. "But there are different types of clouds that bring rain. There are stratocumulus clouds that simply cover the sky, blot out the sun and shower rain. They are not menacing at all. Then there are the cumulonimbus or thunderclouds, which you see up there. Rain does not really require a thundercloud. It is, again, like our own love natures, like parental love, or love between couples. There is nourishment, but often there is also a lot more, as in a thundercloud. How many times have you had a fight with Peter in the name of love? You can see both stratocumulus and cumulonimbus clouds reflected in our lives."

"All right. But earlier you were also saying that thunder-clouds represented war?"

Aliyah thought about that for a moment.

"Well, they seem to represent our conflicts, which on large scales could be seen as war. The conflict could be internal, between couples, in a family, or in a larger arena. But if you think about it, wars have often led to dramatic, positive changes at the level of a culture or a nation, or even the earth. I mean they have created new growth, as historians can testify.

And they have also destroyed things: flooded, sunk, washed them away, or whatever term you like to use."

Emma was again silent.

Aliyah gazed up into the sky at the menacing cumulo-nimbus. Presently she asked,

"Emma, have you heard the name, Thor?"

"Isn't he some kind of pagan god?"

"Yes. Thor, the Norse god of thunder. He is supposed to wield this great hammer. When he hurls it, the hammer causes thunder and lightning. Or so the mythology goes…"

"Think he's still up there?" teased Emma.

"No, silly! But it is indeed a curious myth. Have you observed the shape of a cumulonimbus? I mean, a thundercloud? There is usually a huge, anvil-like shape on the top." Aliyah pointed skyward.

"An anvil? On a thunder cloud?"

"Yes. The legend of Thor probably has a lot to do with it. An anvil is a blacksmith's forging tool. You place a red-hot metal object on the anvil and then hit it hard with a hammer. There is a loud noise, and sparks fly. So if there is all this thunder and lightning, and you see a huge anvil in the sky…"

"There must be some god up there who must be using his hammer! That does make sense. Primitive man worshipped forces of nature, made gods out of them."

"Thor is also portrayed as a god who is constantly at war. It does suit our analogy, doesn't it?"

"I say it does," acknowledged Emma, now straining hard to see the road ahead. The storm seemed to be growing worse. The roar of the winds and the rain and the claps of thunder were deafening. Did a war sound much different? she wondered. And what did the existence of such analogies mean? Then a thought struck her and her eyebrows furrowed.

"Aliyah, even if such correspondences can be true, why should they exist together at the same time? Perhaps the earth-wind-fire-water thingamajig, as you called it, does have some parallels with our lives. But that doesn't mean that these parallels need to exist together at the same time, or even exist at all. But here we are, seeing your analogies side by side, as if one causes the other. You can't really be saying that it is human nature that creates storm clouds, or vice versa. That's too far-fetched."

Aliyah understood what Emma was pointing to. She replied:

"I guess what it means is that either one causes the other, or there is a common, deeper principle at work behind both."

"That is an outrageous suggestion if you ask me!" Emma frowned. "There is literally nothing physical or scientific in common between our natures and the storm, for example. So how can one cause the other? And forget your common principle!"

Aliyah was silent. How, indeed, could such analogies exist? Was it simply her imagination? Again she considered her assumptions. Earth, water, wind and fire, corresponding to body, emotions, mind and spirit. Other than exploring possible relationships between these two realms, perhaps she could explore relationships within the same realm and see how they correspond to the other realm? This sounded like a possible way to validate her postulates further.

What was the relationship between earth, water, wind and fire? For one, they represented solid, liquid, gaseous and plasma states of matter: the earth element being solid, water being liquid, air being gaseous, and fire being heat and light or plasma, such as in the sun. Again, she analyzed the correspondences. It seemed it was not sufficient to consider water as representing emotions. It had to be the liquid state itself that represented emotions. The liquid fossil fuels pointed to that. The mind then could be associated with the gaseous states, not just air. And the solid state represented the physical, such as the body. For an analogy, this made sense, since there were various types of liquids and gases, just as there were various types of emotions and thoughts. The plasma state or fire, then, represented the so-called spirit.

She mused on their interaction as she remembered her high school physics and the phase transitions of matter. The action of heat on solid matter first turned it into a liquid, then a gas, then finally into plasma such as in the sun. Here she found a parallel in physical evolution, for it started with the raw metabolism of physical sustenance such as in the bacteria and single-celled creatures, then became emotions or feelings such as pain, fear, happiness and aggression in animals, and then acquired a mind in higher animals, which reached its pinnacle in man. Similar to the solid, liquid and gaseous transitions, the physical, emotional and mental evolutionary transitions did occur on the earth. The next in the evolutionary progression seemed to be the unfolding of spirit, if that system of analogy were true. The evolutionary transitions, in some ways, corresponded to the phase transitions of matter, and were the result of major changes or leaps in the physiology of an organism. The fossil records on the earth did show dramatic changes in evolutionary development, which couldn't really be explained well by theories of slow change or gradual progression. It seemed that her notions still appeared valid.

Emma was doubtful. "The next step in evolution is the spirit? This is beginning to sound like New Age stuff to me. I do agree that your observations have some grounding, but I do not agree that there can be a common principle behind them. That sounds totally out of this world. Next you will be telling me that God is sitting up there in the sky looking down at us."

Did her theory postulate anything about God at all? The phase transitions of matter were accomplished by applying heat. The sun's heat and light had been the primary causative factor in evolution, supplying the energy that drove physical evolution to what it is today, even providing mutations. The sun itself being in the plasma state corresponding to spirit, she wondered, did this mean that there was an analogous spiritual power source driving evolution through body, emotion and mind into the spirit?

Her eyes widened as she gazed at the setting sun. The earth's origin was intimately connected with the sun, as she knew from astronomy, and all life was sustained by the sun. This was similar to the concept held about God by those of religious beliefs. And if her postulates were true, the sun had to be an analogue of God, if God did exist. Wasn't that also true in the analogy of the solar system that came to her in a dream?

This was an amazing correlation. It struck Aliyah so hard that it took her breath away for a moment, but doubt and healthy skepticism returned quickly. Nevertheless she found herself asking,

"Emma, do you think there's a real..." her voice trailed off.

"You mean Thor?" Emma smiled, turning to look at her friend.

Before Aliyah could reply, a big flash came from outside, lighting up the car, followed by a loud honk. Emma screamed and hit the brakes, turning the wheel furiously. The car screeched, swerved hard and exited the road, bumping up and down.

"Look out!" Aliyah yelled as the vehicle careened in semi-darkness towards a big boulder. Emma again swerved hard to the right and the Beetle came screeching to a halt. Then they heard a muffled crashing sound.

"Crazy idiot!" raged Emma, "Came out of thin air! I'll bet he thinks he owns this place!"

Aliyah breathed again, "That was really close! We could have been killed!"

They sat is silence, contemplating their narrow escape. Emma went pale, considering what might have happened, and she stared at the wheel blankly.

Aliyah knew the look and took her hand. "The important thing is that we are still in one piece. Not sure I can say the same about whoever went flying by!"

She peered outside through the windshield. She thought she could see smoke rising.

"He must have been blind or drunk!" Emma found her anger again. "Or stoned!"

"Well you can say that again, literally! Whoever it is appears to have crashed. We'd better help."

43

"Oh, no, I am not going out there! Who knows what kind of psycho we have run into in the middle of the desert? Let's get out of here!"

Emma released the brakes and hit the gas pedal. The engine revved.

"But we can't just leave the scene of an accident!"

Emma stared at her friend, and then outside. She was now thinking considerably more about what had happened, and her face turned anxious. She looked to her left.

"I can't get out. There is a boulder blocking my door."

She tried the gas pedal again. The engine revved but the car would not move.

"Okay, stop. I'll take a look."

"Stay put, Aliyah! We don't know who or what is out there! Didn't you see how it came out of nowhere?" Emma sounded frantic.

"It? You've been watching too many movies! That who or what could be injured, even dying!"

"Not this one!" cried Emma as she peered out through the windshield. Rain was beating down hard. Then she let out a shriek,

"Oh, no! It's coming this way!"

"It?"

"No, he! With an ax! Or is it a hammer? Lock your window Aliyah, quick!"

Emma hit the gas again, revving the engine hard. But the car seemed to be fully stuck. She tried the reverse, but that didn't work either.

She turned to Aliyah, her face white. "What shall we do?"

The dark, menacing figure outside approached the window slowly, stopped and regarded them silently for a moment. Then came the sound of metal tapping glass, twice.

"Well, whoever it is doesn't scare me…" said Aliyah. She rolled down the window, thrust her head out into the rain and shouted:

"Hi, I'm Aliyah…"

Her voice trailed off as she found herself looking into the steely muzzle of a rifle and then at a tall figure gazing down at her. Lightning flashed and she saw the rugged face of a man. He had long hair falling to his shoulders.

They weighed each other in silence.

Then an icy voice cut through the tumult of the storm: "I am Thor."

5. Car

Aliyah discovers that totally different realms could have common principles behind them.

The rain started thinning out and the winds grew calmer. The storm was dwindling fast. Aliyah stared in consternation at the dark figure outside. For a moment, she was literally blown away, but managed to recover her wits quickly. Now she looked down at the rifle and felt a rising fire of anger within.

"Scared to death of unarmed women, aren't you?" she said sweetly, with all the sarcasm she could muster.

The rifle lowered, but still pointed toward the car. She could sense some discomfort in the stranger's gaze.

"I don't take kindly to hit-and-run drivers, ma'm. Not in this place." His voice was polite but icy.

47

The rain thinned down to a drizzle and the light became brighter. The man appeared to be in his early thirties and had crease lines on his forehead.

"Hit and run?" She was getting angrier, but continued smiling. "You came flying too low, if I remember right. Don't they have any traffic signs up there?"

Her jibe seemed to have no effect.

"You came right at me, ma'm," he replied sternly, "as though you did it on purpose. Otherwise, you two must have been yapping, or drunk, or both."

She had really wanted to help and now here was this man accusing them of attacking him and trying to get away. With effort, she bit down her anger and turned to look at her friend.

Emma finally found her voice.

"I'm sorry!" she called out. "It was all my fault. I am really not used to driving in this weather. It really scares me."

The man said nothing and continued to look intently at them.

"My car seems to be stuck in mud. How about yours?" Emma tried again.

Aliyah glared at her friend. Playing the damsel in distress was not to her liking.

"It's a wreck," he replied curtly without turning his head. "There is no way it can get me to where I am headed."

"Would it be fine if we drop you at the nearest service station?" Emma sounded very polite.

The man hesitated for a moment. Then he said briskly, "Open the trunk, ma'm. If I find what I suspect, you and your gracious friend here will be making a long trek tonight."

"Be careful," Aliyah told him, "our pet rattler likes it there in the trunk."

Aliyah felt a jab on her side. The man ignored the comment and moved cautiously to the back of the car, still keeping them covered with the rifle.

"Keep your eyes front," he called out.

Emma quickly unlatched the trunk. They could hear him rummaging around inside and they exchanged glances. He seemed to be looking for something. Soon the back door snap shut.

He was again near the window, looking down curiously at them. The rifle was now held loose, pointing to the ground.

"You girls from the university?"

"That's right, sir. Have you ever been to one?" Aliyah flashed.

He ignored the question.

"What are you doing out here in the wilderness? You know, this is a dangerous place, not exactly where girls go looking for their next party."

"It's a free country, sir. We do run into some vermin once in a while. Nothing we can't handle," Aliyah replied meaningly.

The man appeared to again ignore the remark. Did he really have a thick skin? she wondered. But before she could say anything else, he tapped on the car and called out to Emma,

"The way she is stuck, she's not going anywhere till the water dries up. But I can get her out of mud, if you put her in neutral."

"I think he means you," Emma grinned as she shifted gears. Aliyah glared at her friend.

The man moved away again. Soon they felt the car shake and then move forward slowly.

"He's a strong one," Emma whispered. "Didn't ask us to get out too. Don't you think he's really a nice and helpful guy?"

"He's helping himself!" shot back Aliyah. "Can't you see that?"

The car shook again and stopped moving.

"Gimme a minute," came the voice from behind. "I'm getting my stuff from the jeep. Besides, I am drenched. Where do you think I could change?"

"Try that one," Aliyah shouted back, and pointed to a cactus patch across the road.

She heard his laughter and quickly managed to parry another nudge from Emma.

"Show some restraint, will you? You could have landed us in big trouble. We're lucky that he's a nice guy."

"Nice??? I'm sorry, Emma. I just don't like people pointing guns at me and ordering me about. That wasn't nice at all."

"Yeah! But I wonder who he thought we were. Drug runners, do you think? They can be dangerous."

"Possibly. But I found his behavior inexcusable."

"You weren't exactly Mother Teresa!" Emma replied, "So pipe down, now."

The man was back in a short while, toting a duffel bag. He had changed into a fresh set of clothes. The gun, which she suspected to have somehow made its way into the bag, had disappeared.

"So you are not making a run for it?" he asked with an impish smile. She thought he looked attractive when he smiled.

"Why did you pull a gun on us?"

He seemed to deliberate for a moment.

"You could say I was expecting company. Guess I should have brought the artillery instead…" He continued to smile.

Aliyah blushed a little and decided not to reply.

Emma emerged from the wayside restaurant, feeling happy and refreshed. The storm had passed over and a cool breeze was blowing.

"Ah! That was good. You gotta love junk food!" She was now in a mood to chatter as they started off again. Except for some occasional friction with Aliyah, the man had turned out to be pleasant company. Though he commonly used the name Thor, his real name was Theodore, and his friends called him Theo. But he consistently refused to give out any more personal information about himself. And that was maddening.

Emma had been hatching up a plan, and she decided to put it into action.

"Now look at that, Aliyah!" she laughed, pointing towards the horizon, where there was still some light left. "Doesn't that cloud look like a flying duck? I suppose you'll tell me now how your newfangled principle makes clouds resemble ducks!"

Aliyah laughed, too. Her train of thought had been sidetracked by their little adventure, but now she got to thinking about it all over again.

Theo suddenly showed interest.

"What principle?" he asked, turning to look at Aliyah.

"Uh, nothing really! Emma is just having fun." she replied.

"Oh, no!" Emma replied. "Aliyah likes to connect clouds with human nature, storms with human nature, deserts with human nature, in fact everything with human nature."

"That sounds interesting," Theo replied thoughtfully. "Why do you call it a 'principle' ?"

"Well, there are some interesting relationships we found. When you keep seeing the same pattern multiple times, it could mean that there is some principle behind it." Aliyah was now getting academic.

"Patterns? What patterns?" Theo's interest seemed genuine.

"So far, so good," Emma said to herself and then continued loudly. "While you two go crazy about it, let me check the traffic situation in the city. We don't want to get stuck for hours in traffic, not if I can help it."

Emma turned on the radio and tuned to a station while Aliyah and Theo talked. The radio coughed and sputtered and the sound came intermittently, broken with noise and squeals. She tried tuning the station repeatedly.

"Dammit," she finally cried out, banging her palm on the radio. "Reception is pretty poor. I am sure I received it well the last time we came through here."

"Perhaps your Beetle needs her antennae fixed," joked Aliyah.

"And perhaps you need yours fixed!" retorted Emma. "The way they seem to drag you to these creepy places."

They both laughed, but Aliyah stopped short as a thought struck her.

"Hey Emma! Why do cars resemble insects or even animals? Don't you see that they are built to give such an appearance with eyes, mouth, and maybe a snout? The four wheels are like four legs, the rear-view mirrors resemble ears, there is a main body that corresponds to the trunk…" She stopped short, and then added, "There is even, hmm… a gluteus maximus."

"You mean ass, don't you?" Emma burst out laughing. "Well, you're right. I hadn't noticed that before."

It seemed that what Aliyah said was true. Her car and most others did have structures that resembled animals. The grill, the headlights, the windshield, tires, side-view mirrors, doors, even the antenna. That was very curious.

"Now that you mention it, there does seem to be a kind of correspondence to animals there. I suppose it is a self-expression by the designers." Emma laughed again, and then paused, "I know what you are saying. You are asking how there exists an analogy between cars and animals without a common principle. Well, I don't know. It looks like there is no explanation other than the influence of a creative mind."

"Well, I think the creative influence is pretty strong there." Theo entered the discussion. "But then I don't think car designers have any conscious desire to make them so."

He paused, reflected and then continued, "Your car does have bodily systems similar to an animal's, doesn't it? There is a skeletal system that holds everything together. There is a muscular system for movement composed of the gears, pistons, transmission and wheels. And there is a digestive system too, ingesting gasoline and converting it into energy."

"Could he be a mechanic?" Aliyah wondered to herself.

"And quite costly food too, the way gas prices are soaring," laughed Emma.

But this was something unexpected. There indeed was some kind of correspondence there, which was more than skin-deep. In addition to a digestive system, there was an excretory system of exhaust gases. Emma tried to recollect her college biology. There was the human nervous system, but was there an analogue in the car?

She didn't want to ask Theo, so she asked Aliyah. But it was Theo who responded.

"Yes, there is. There are many feedback control and correction systems within the car, to regulate speed, and control braking and traction. Now with computers on board, you really do have a proper autonomic nervous system. Your steering wheel and pedals for braking and acceleration are part of the car's nervous system too. Only its nerves are wires and cables. But what it lacks is a conscious brain, which is, of course, provided by you, the driver."

"I wonder how much *that* contributes," replied Aliyah. She did not like the way Emma had set her up.

"Well, I don't have to be an intellectual. Looking nice and pretty is my thing," Emma laughed again.

"So is your car," Aliyah observed. "You take good care of its integumentary system. If you don't know what that is, it refers to the skin. Your car has a beautiful skin, and even a theft deterrent sensor on it."

Emma obviously liked the analogy, for she laughed hard.

Then she thought of something else. "But animals breathe. Cars don't," she objected.

"Hmm, that's true. But wait..." replied Theo this time, "The combustion in the engine requires oxygen doesn't it? That's the same thing that happens in our cells when we breathe. Oxygen releases the energy held in sugars. In the car, it releases energy held in the fuel. And there's more! Aren't both gasoline and sugars carbon- and hydrogen-based? Gasoline is based on hydrocarbons. And our food is mostly carbohydrates! The energy driving the body is indeed taken from breaking down carbon and hydrogen chains. And both the body and the car release carbon dioxide and water as waste! So you see, the car does breathe like us!"

"He can't be a mechanic," Aliyah said to herself.

"Well, that's not quite the bodily chemistry that I am used to!" laughed Emma. "But I must say it is pretty curious. Hmm. Now it's almost like I am riding an animal. I suppose that's how it would appear to a caveman."

"Yes, indeed," breathed Aliyah. "But why?"

She puzzled for a while as she tried to analyze the correspondence. Was there a deeper principle at work that provided a common ground? She thought of what Emma had said. To a caveman, a moving car would indeed look like a live animal. But the similarity was not just in the appearance, but in its systems too. Then something clicked, and she found it very curious!

"Emma, there *is* a common principle. You see, life, as biologists define it, is essentially metabolism. You know what that term means?"

"I think so, but refresh my memory, will you?"

"Well, it represents chemical and physical processes in the body. They take in energy sources from the environment, break them down to release energy, and use that energy for various functions. The waste products are released back into the environment. Anything *alive* as defined by biologists needs to have systems that perform such tasks. Even bacteria have rudimentary systems that do these. So what we are looking at is a life-giving principle or a blueprint, as architects call it."

From the corner of her eye, she saw Theo look at her curiously.

"Now you are going way over my head," said Emma, "You don't mean to say that my car is alive, do you? I've seen some movies like that where they have a mind of their own."

"No, no, that's not what I mean at all. That's just fiction. Life need not be associated with sentient intelligence, at least not to biologists. Bacteria are not intelligent, and I don't think worms have any thinking capacity. Your car is obviously not alive, as we recognize life. But it seems to be a kind of embodiment of a life-giving blueprint, so that it gives the appearance of life."

"Blueprint?"

"Look at it this way. When scientists look for life on the earth or elsewhere in the universe, they expect to see bodies with supportive structures, muscular structures, digestive apparatus, sensors and so on. The tasks these structures do are essential ingredients for deriving energy, for moving around and functioning. And, in fact, many biologists equate these processes with life. Then the car is something that you may call proto-life. It is a type of manifestation of a deeper principle of life."

Theo looked impressed, and she felt a strange wave of happiness.

"Aliyah, I am still trying to understand you. What do you mean by proto-life?" Emma was not about to give up.

"Well, it simply means that for any physical entity to sustain itself over long periods of time, it requires a set of systems in place, such as we see in the human body. Possibly evolution has discovered and applied these into our internal systems. The designer of a car also has to build the same systems. He or she has no need to wait for evolution to discover them. The systems may look different and vary in complexity, but many principles behind them are the same. So things like cars, trucks and other automobiles which are built on the same principles, could then be considered to be artificial life forms. That is what I meant by proto-life."

Theo was now silent, looking away into the distance. She wondered what he was thinking about. He probably found it all too much to handle.

Emma considered this new piece of information. Indeed, a car was somewhat like a horse. Besides the riding, one had to feed it, house it, wash and groom it, even take it to a "vet" once in a while, as if it were alive. "Really! I could compare it to an animal or insect in a poetic sense, but the association is deeper," she said to herself. Was it possible that many analogies do have some common principles behind them, as Aliyah was saying? Was poetic inspiration or intuitive recognition a sub-conscious discovery of deep connections?

"So you are saying that analogies exist because of common principles?" she asked. "That was your point, wasn't it? That a single principle can manifest in different areas, resulting in analogies of one another?"

"More or less. When the analogies are deep, they definitely smack of common ground."

Theo seemed to agree, for she saw him smile and gently nod his head. Again, she felt strangely elated.

A brief silence ensued as Aliyah fell back into her world of thoughts. Emma, driving her Beetle, now evoked a different picture in her mind. It pointed to an analogous phenomenon at the level of body, mind and spirit – that of a soul inhabiting and driving bodily systems. And this was as amazing a correlation as she had discovered about the sun!

The car turned onto University Avenue and headed towards the biological sciences building. Theo had requested that he be dropped off there, saying he wanted to visit a friend.

"First time to the university, is it?" Aliyah enquired.

"Yes," Theo agreed.

"Thought so!" she jibed. 'Well, try not to make any trouble here. We do have road signs everywhere, that is, if you decide to follow them!"

Emma flashed her a look. Theo said nothing, but pointed to the building up ahead and said, "Drop me off there, please, next to the entrance."

A floodlight towered over the entrance, where a man stood idly watching the street. The car came to a stop and Theo stepped out. He turned to thank them both when a loud and boisterous voice came sailing through the air.

"Professor Thor! So glad to see you! We were expecting you next week. And we all heard about your adventure in Egypt!"

The dean of arts & sciences walked briskly towards Theo, his right hand outstretched.

Aliyah cringed.

6. Sky

Aliyah finds a reflection of the mind and the search for enlightenment, in the atmosphere that surrounds the earth.

The days seemed to stretch endlessly, turning slowly into weeks and months. Aliyah struggled through her studies, her assignments and other coursework. Despite all her efforts and attention, a dangerous emotion of abject meaninglessness overpowered her at times. It came particularly during those times when she found herself bored, with nothing to do, and the feeling of desperation that arose in those moments was so intense that it wrought literal soul suffering. She was scared to confront it, afraid that those moments might develop into a burning conflagration that would consume her completely.

The same moments seemed to invade her sleeping hours as well. They came occasionally during early mornings, when she was in a twilight zone of consciousness. The dreams would fade and she would be half asleep, half awake. During such times, she could suddenly move into a nether world of pure consciousness, where nothing existed but herself. She could not feel her body, and there was nothing to see, hear or sense in any way. There was only a focused consciousness, existing somewhere in time, and all alone, in what appeared to be an absolute dark void. These were moments of terror when she came face to face with herself as a being, when she could not focus attention on anything else to escape those deep emotions that lurked within. She felt completely lost and in agony, as her origins and the very meaning of her existence were challenged.

And it had its impact. She had ignored consciousness per se, taken it for granted and had never bothered about what it meant. Now here it was, giving her some moments of literal agony. Emma suggested that it probably resulted from some major trauma in her early life. It could even be associated with her birth, a long and painful labor, she had been told, during which her mother had expired. She toyed with the idea of a regression session with a psychiatrist, to identify and relive traumatic events as a cathartic process, but then changed her mind. She was now very curious about consciousness itself, and she sought to understand it better through whatever means she could. And here she had her own backyard to play in. It took courage but she was determined to take a closer look. After all, that might accomplish the cleansing that she needed.

Then by chance, or so it seemed, she was introduced to some eastern meditation techniques through a friend. These techniques dealt with consciousness and the mind, and how meditation could still the mind and reveal deeper states within. She found the concepts fascinating and soon found herself studying them intensely and practicing some of the techniques. She was then introduced to the concept of enlightenment, which was the ultimate goal, it taught, of every human being.

It seemed a worthwhile pursuit, for she felt she had nothing to lose.

This then was her goal, as she invested herself whole-heartedly into her spiritual practices. At first her efforts seemed futile, but soon her meditation and exercises started yielding results, for she went into deeper and deeper silence and introspection. The emotions of loneliness and terror that she felt during her early mornings mellowed considerably and soon disappeared as she slowly came to terms with herself. They were soon replaced by a gentle silence of being that seemed to grow deeper and deeper. And they even started stealing in, not just in the night, but during her waking hours of meditation as well. She could move into such a state of pure consciousness and silence within her being after she had immersed herself for some time in meditation. This helped immensely in her studies, as she renewed herself during these times, being able to focus and apply herself well to whatever she wanted to do.

And she basked in the pond of Basho, and the haikus and koans of various masters. They were the keys to cross the barriers in the layers of the mind. Life, she held, was unknown and unknowable. One could only be like the white clouds floating in the skies, enjoying the mystery of what will always remain mysterious. There was no sense in asking why, for there could be no answers, no ultimate purposes. The questioner, she insisted, disappears with the question in an enlightened consciousness. She had finally found contentment. And enlightenment, she thought, was not far away.

But life always deals with contentment, and oft times quite forcefully. Aliyah found herself losing command of her thoughts and emotions as they started going out of control, focusing more and more elsewhere. Her meditation was thrown into havoc and she started losing grip on herself. Then came an emotion that literally set her afire, threw her senses into disarray, and drove her mad, as she sought to regain her control and composure. She was falling deeply in love.

"You are... what do you call... a preceptor?" Lisa looked her in the eye.

"Sort of," Aliyah smiled. "The Master will be here in an hour or so. I am holding the fort till then."

Lisa turned towards Theo, "I'm so sorry, honey! I was sure that you could meet the Master himself. We'll come some other time..."

"I don't have much time for this sort of stuff. I'm here only because you insisted," Theo smiled. "But I'm sure Aliyah would do just as well."

"You know her?" Lisa sounded surprised.

"Well, sort of." Theo sounded defensive. "I did tell you, if you remember."

Lisa raised her eyebrows and turned to look at Aliyah.

"Oh, so you are the one!" she whistled. "Wrecked his jeep and ruined my date! And preaching about some high principle too, of all the nonsense!"

"Actually, it was an accident. I believe we were all at fault," Aliyah smiled gently.

"That's what they all say," Lisa countered. "The worst part was that his head seemed to be stuck in the clouds for a while after that."

Theo looked embarrassed. "Well, I did describe your notions to Lisa. It was kind of interesting..."

Aliyah felt a thrill of joy, but kept her reserve. She was excited to meet Theo again, though embarrassed as well because of the previous incident. She had heard a lot about him recently, from her own discreet inquiries and from his reputation as an adventurer.

"Yeah! Some God principle!" Lisa had coined a word, "There's too much pseudo-science and bogus spirituality floating around."

"Well, it's something I am still researching," Aliyah replied, leading them into the inner garden of the building where they could sit down.

"It doesn't need much research to figure out, does it?" Lisa asked meaningly.

Aliyah did not answer.

"See, you teach people how to transcend the mind. Now if mind is like air, I suppose the analogy is, what shall I say, you choke them to death?" Lisa laughed heartily.

"That is funny," Aliyah agreed, "though not quite what I had in mind."

"Ah, so you do have something in mind," Theo smiled. "I'd like to hear it."

"Well, if you really want to…" Aliyah smiled back at him.

Lisa did not look pleased. "How about coming back later when the Master is here? It's almost time for lunch."

"We'll wait for him," said Theo. "Meanwhile I'm sure Aliyah can tell us something about the mind… or what she has in mind."

Aliyah suddenly felt cornered. She really wanted to discuss her thoughts with Theo, but felt that Lisa would turn into a vehement opponent. A confrontation was not to her liking.

"Perhaps we could discuss this another time?" she looked at Theo. His eyes were fixed intently on hers, and she felt that he liked the suggestion very much.

"I think now is as good a time as any," Lisa, who did not like the idea at all, intervened quickly. "I believe you were going to tell us about the mind?"

"Okay," Aliyah nodded as she motioned them to sit down. "Would you like some tea first?"

Sunlight poured from the top of the open courtyard and painted the garden in a curious mix of light and shade. The interior of the wooden building held what was known as a garden of meditation. Rocks and pebbles arranged in peculiar patterns on uneven terrain helped many who contemplated them to attain deeper states of consciousness.

Aliyah looked on silently at the rocks while Lisa and Theo sipped green tea. Lisa did not seem to like her drink, for she made a face. Theo appeared silent in his thoughts.

"The mind, as the Master says," Aliyah began, "is layered much like an onion. And it is possible to navigate those layers in meditation…"

"What do you mean, layers?" asked Theo.

"Well, the layering is a perception. As you go deeper into meditation, there are various shifts in consciousness. The quality of these states varies, and one state is different from another. You go past these layers, entering deeper and deeper into meditation."

"I see. What happens then?"

"Well, that's what is most interesting. After peeling layer after layer, nothing remains."

"What?" Theo sounded incredulous.

"Nothing that one would call as mind. It is absolute stillness and void. Even your 'I' does not exist in that state."

Lisa cut in impatiently. "I know all these from the Master's teachings. But how does it have anything to do with your suppositions?"

"Well, the analogy is not very difficult to find," Aliyah responded.

"The only one that comes to my mind is hot air!" Lisa was distinctively aggressive.

"The atmosphere perhaps?" Theo intervened with a curious smile.

"Yes!" Aliyah smiled back, glad that Theo was following her line of thought. "The earth's atmosphere is also layered and seems to have some curious correspondence with the mind."

Indeed, the earth's atmosphere was layered like an onion. Most of the activity of wind and weather were at the bottom-most layer called the troposphere. Here existed most of the weather phenomena, and its currents breathed life into the earth and carried around the creative potential of life in pollen and seeds. The currents whipped ocean waves into a frenzy, moved water as vapor through the air, brought cold or warm spells, created tornadoes and storms, and determined seasons. Here was to be found reflections of the typical human mind with its creativity, and its uncontrolled and often forceful thought patterns, driving emotions into passions and resulting in physical activity.

Theo found the description interesting, but voiced a concern. "The mind is the most creative faculty that we have. All of civilization is built and driven by the mind. It cannot be trivialized by a simple analogy."

"True, the mind is the builder. The Master says that mind influences and even creates matter. In some philosophies, existence is an appearance in consciousness, did you know?"

"I know that," replied Lisa laughing. "So you are now going to describe how hot air creates everything?"

Aliyah wondered why Lisa was so aggressive with her, almost jealous. But the question deserved an answer. She reached out her hand and swept it gently through the bush next to her.

"It's amazing isn't it? To think that this bush is a condensation of air?"

"What?" Lisa thought she was being ridiculed.

"No, really! This plant is indeed precipitated out of thin air. Its body mass is composed mostly of carbon, taken from carbon dioxide in the air."

Lisa simply stared.

"Interesting! How much of it comes from the air, do you know?" This from Theo.

"I spent some time studying it," Aliyah smiled. "Carbon dioxide contributes about ninety-three percent, hydrogen from water about seven percent and minerals from the ground less than a fraction of a percentage!"

"Now this is really far out..." Lisa started.

"No, she's right!" Theo agreed. "Plants get most of their body mass from the air. There's even a technique of farming known as aeroponics where plants are grown in air, without soil. And water, composed of hydrogen and oxygen, is a precipitation of these common gases in the air."

"All right! So there is some correspondence with air and mind when it comes to plants. But I didn't precipitate out of thin air!" Lisa objected.

"But your food comes from plants, or animals that ate plants. So one could argue that almost all biomass on the earth is made from thin air!" replied Aliyah.

"That is definitely interesting, but your inference seems incomplete," said Theo. "It takes photosynthesis to create the body of a plant. That means sunlight, water and minerals too. It's the sun's energy that makes food what it is and sustains life on the planet, isn't it?"

"True! Minerals help create enzymes that build the body of the plant. Their role is more like construction workers," she replied. "The Sun represents the fire element or spirit. So photosynthesis then points to the action of spirit where it combines with mind, emotions and matter to manifest all life!"

Lisa looked bored. But Theo seemed to find it quite interesting.

"I see. So your take is that the sustaining energy of life ultimately comes from spirit; mind and emotions are the source of manifestation; matter is the crucible. Is that a fair statement?"

"More or less. Photosynthesis by analogy represents the very essence of creation and life, not only from a biological viewpoint, but also from a higher level!"

"I don't believe a word of it," scoffed Lisa.

"I almost don't either," laughed Theo. "But true or not, it is an interesting proposition. Please go on…"

"There isn't much to tell." Aliyah felt a little snubbed.

"Oh, yes, there is!" smiled Theo. "I can't imagine Aliyah giving up at this point!"

"Well, there is a bit more, I guess." She blushed a little and continued. "So far, we were discussing the troposphere. Now going further up, one comes across a kind of barrier called the tropopause. This segregates the air below and that above through a temperature inversion. Quite like the barriers that you feel while trying to meditate, you know, quieting ourselves down, trying to reign in all this barrage of thoughts. But once you manage it, you quickly enter a calmer state of mind."

"I know what you are talking about. It's not very easy to still the mind," Lisa agreed, "but once you do it, you are at peace."

Aliyah was thankful that Lisa now appeared less belligerent.

"Yes," she agreed. "Above the tropopause, things really quieten down. Air currents, clouds and thunderstorms are left behind. Instead of temperature continuing to decrease, it actually increases. This layer is called the stratosphere."

"Yeah! My boyfriend is sometimes found there!" laughed Lisa, nudging Theo.

"And here you find the protective ozone layer," Aliyah continued. "It is above this that you find what may be called other-worldly phenomena; incursions and visitations from outer-space, like meteors, comets, cosmic rays, radiation…"

"So in the stratosphere you have the analogy of the calm, quiet mind. Beyond that, you start experiencing something new?"

"That's true. The ozone layer is also a protective layer. Likewise, there also appears to be a shield in the layers of mind that prevents extraneous influences from reaching into ordinary levels of our consciousness. The layers beyond this can prove to be strange, even dangerous."

"I see, so what happens above the stratosphere?"

Going up past layers and barriers, one reached so high that a glance below revealed a new dimension to the earth, the hidden splendors of the beautiful tapestry that it really was. Here one stood apart and watched the earth in wonder, just as in higher states the mind became so calm and serene that one could observe life with a new, unified and wondrous perspective. Indeed, those who have been lucky enough to view the earth from space have always found their perceptions forever changed.

Climbing yet higher, one entered the ionosphere. Here the action of strong, unfiltered sunlight literally tore apart electrons from their very atoms and molecules, and everything in this layer existed as charged ions. Even water could not exist in its vapor form. Density was extremely low, and the rarefied atmosphere existed in a high state of vibration, electric in nature. Here occurred the beautiful phenomenon of aurora borealis or the northern lights, as charged emissions from the sun entered the ionosphere, creating dazzling displays. The corresponding analogy in the mind was obvious. The ionosphere represented a very deep state in the mind, rarefied and of a very high vibration, where thoughts ceased and the mind existed in an electric-like or spiritual state. The aurora borealis reminded her of beauteous experiences that sometimes occurred in such deeper states of the mind, originating in a spiritual source represented by the Sun. And indeed, the ionized state of this level and these charged emissions were considered to be examples of the plasma state of matter, which, by analogy, represented the spirit.

Beyond the ionosphere was the exosphere where the atmosphere was so rarefied that it merged into outer space and soon ceased to be. This she considered to be a state where mind ceased to exist, merging in an apparent void. All that was present was a magnificent spiritual source represented by the Sun, which bathed her in its eternal light. She likened this to enlightenment. Moving from the very ground that represented earthly life, up to the heavens through the atmosphere, till only the Sun was left to experience, here was a perfect analogy of entering deeper and deeper into meditation, transcending the mind layer by layer, till she found enlightenment. After peeling the onion of mind layer after layer, it ceased to exist. *Once again, the Sun had become an analogue of the ultimate spiritual source!*

Her phone rang all of a sudden. Aliyah apologized for the interruption and took the call. Presently she announced,

"The Master apologizes for not being here in person. He had to leave urgently. Said he'll be in tomorrow, if you would like to meet him."

"That's okay," replied Theo. "We'll meet him some other time. We really have to leave now."

"Yes," yawned Lisa, "and thank you, dear, for the engaging conversation. You should think of writing it down some day."

"Not a bad idea!" agreed Theo. He reached into his wallet and pulled out a card. "Here's my business card. Feel free to call me if you need any help with your research."

Lisa flashed him a dark look, but said nothing.

Aliyah took the proffered card and thanked them both for their visit. Inwardly, she felt elated. Not only had Theo listened to her seriously, he had even asked her to call him if she liked. He must be impressed, particularly with her knowledge of meditation.

She watched Lisa and Theo leave and then went over to her room to pick up her things. Tucking away Theo's card carefully into one of her books, she decided that she would find some excuse to call him soon. She turned and looked out the window to see if he were still around.

Lisa and Theo were in the parking lot, partly hidden by the trees. Lisa had her arms around his neck and they were kissing passionately. For a moment, Aliyah stared, then quickly turned away. She felt a stabbing pain within, accompanied by waves of dissatisfaction and frustration. Recognizing the feeling as dangerous, she quickly sat down, controlled her breathing and soon entered into a state of meditative absorption. Her efforts succeeded, for when she came out of the state, the pain had vanished. But oddly enough, there remained a quiet, throbbing discontent.

This discontent was soon to turn into an obsession.

For was life unknown and purposeless? If intelligence and consciousness existed at its foundation, then everything had to have meaning and purpose. Aliyah had not yet experienced the Sun, even though she had journeyed far into the upper realms. It was as though she had always been on the *night side* of the atmosphere, one devoid of light, meaning and purpose, where the height of all experience was the Void, a cessation of all experience.

Studying her analogies, she suspected that there existed a *day side* to the same realm, but on the other side, one of unimaginable light, power and beauty. And she did not quite know how to get there. Now the earth below was calling her down, a pull that she could not escape.

7. Rhythm

Aliyah maps the movement of the heavens to life on earth.

The motion was incessant, regular, rhythmic, and determined. The circle of movement completed itself many times over, returning to its origins each time, only to begin itself anew. Did it lay to waste each of its cycles through meaningless repetition? Nay, each onward movement and return always contributed something new, accumulated experience and provided an impetus to another motion of a greater order, providing the latter its momentum to move forward. The incessant cyclic rhythm thus created a higher rhythm in that greater order, which, too, completed itself time

69

and again, returning to its origins over vast periods of time - to start all over again. Even this great rhythm gave of itself to an even greater one that spanned ages, and so on to higher levels that embraced eons and unspoken time scales, till time itself vanished into the timeless.

Emma threw down the magazine in disgust. "Would you believe it? It says here that Librans will find romance and intimacy this week. And I just broke up with Peter! What kind of an idiot dreams up all this balderdash? What a load of baloney!"

Aliyah looked up from her desk and said softly, "I am sorry about your boyfriend."

But Emma seemed nonchalant. She had been through this before, or perhaps knew Peter better.

"Oh, bother him! Good riddance! But I know you've been studying this nonsense for months now. What have you got to say about this?"

"What would you like to know?" Aliyah smiled. "Like how long it would take for Peter to show up with apologies and flowers?"

'That will be the day!" Emma grimaced. "He can't tell a rose from a chrysanthemum! But that's not what I asked you," she continued. "Why are you dragging yourself into this hocus pocus weirdo stuff? Are you finally getting serious about this guy?"

Aliyah refused to fully acknowledge that her heart strings had literally pulled her into her new pastime.

"Oh, this is just an interesting hobby, nothing more," she explained.

Emma was not deceived, "Yeah? So how come you run off to him frequently these days? Think you can get him to give you his birthdate and time?"

Aliyah took a mock swipe at her head. Emma ducked and they both giggled like children.

"Well, maybe!" acknowledged Aliyah. "But I do find there is some truth in these planetary rhythms and their effect on people. I've been doing some analysis."

"C'mon girl, be serious. Are you telling me that these planets zillions of miles away from the earth control my personal life? Give me a break!"

"Whoever said they control your life? That would be the most ridiculous conclusion to make."

Emma was confused. "If you think so, then why are you reading all this stuff? I see you doing calculations and making doodles, those things you call charts. What did you find in them that is scientifically valid?"

"Well, I've done some trials and I've found something that might interest you too. But tell me, why did you break up with Peter?"

"Why didn't I break up with him earlier, you mean?" Emma fumed. "The bum kept me waiting for an eternity at the café by the waterfront. Didn't show up until an hour later, and not a single phone call either! And this is not the first time, I tell you! That's the classic Peter!"

"So you had a fight?"

"If you call making a scene 'fighting', yes! And do you know, this time he had the silliest of all excuses? He said his watch stopped! I got so mad..."

Aliyah's eyes widened, "Really, so he did not make his appointment because of his watch? Very curious!"

"Curious? Curious? That's all you've got to say?" Emma exclaimed. "The idiot ruins every plan I make!"

On she went, triggered by Aliyah's response, giving voice to some choice expletives and phrases that helped let off some steam. And finally she quieted down.

Aliyah smiled, for she knew this was just another fight between Emma and Peter. "But it *is* curious Emma! Look at your watch, or at that wall clock for a moment. Do you see those hands? Would you say that they control your life?"

"Control my life? What do you mean? Well I do keep time, and I hate being tardy."

"Still if you think about it, don't those hands have magical powers?" Aliyah was laughing. "They wake up people in the morning, put them to sleep at night, drag many to their offices, make people meet one another, force them into all kinds of activities... Now don't you think that's magic? The very orientation of those hands has so much power over us!"

"Now you are laughing at me! What is your point? You know very well that clocks have no magical powers. All of us simply order our lives around them. So what's the big deal?"

"Well, you just described the astrological system. The clock does carry a good reflection of it. The planets do not control you any more or any less than those hands do. As with the clock, any appearance of control is by arrangement and by agreement. It is all about making and meeting appointments."

Emma sat down heavily. "Appointments? What do you mean appointments? And explain yourself on whatever you just said about my watch."

"Let's take the last one first. Tell me this. How many digits are there on your watch?"

"Twelve, silly!"

"And how many are the astrological signs, the signs of the zodiac?"

"Twelve," answered Emma shortly. "But that is just a coincidence."

"Perhaps. Now let us take the hands. You have the hour hand, the minute hand and the seconds hand. Can you guess what they represent?"

"How should I know? I mean, they of course tell time, but what else?"

"The seconds hand is the fastest moving hand, and it makes a full round through the twelve digits much faster than the others. Now if you think about the solar system and the earth, the seconds hand making a round through the twelve digits corresponds to the earth rotating on its own axis. In doing so, an observer on the earth sees all the twelve zodiac signs in one rotation. That is, the celestial sky around the solar system in one quick cycle."

"Hmm, that is an interesting observation. But how does that relate to astrology?"

"Well, astrological systems map the zodiac against the place and time where one is born. That is, the position of the planets against the zodiac at the time of your birth, but as viewed from your birthplace. This is an earth-centric view. As the earth makes a full rotation, the zodiac with all the planets and the Sun would appear to make a full rotation around the earth."

"You are saying that the seconds hand represents the earth's rotation, moving through the twelve zodiac signs."

"That would be a close description. This movement seen in the skies is divided into twelve divisions in astrology, called the twelve houses. You can then compare the seconds hand rotation through the twelve digits, to the heavens and the planets moving through the twelve houses as the earth makes one rotation about its axis."

"Whatever! And what about the minute hand? I suppose that corresponds to the earth's revolution around the sun?"

"You guessed it right. It takes many rotations of the seconds hand before the minute hand makes a full rotation. Likewise it takes many rotations of the earth around its axis, before it makes a full circle around the Sun. And as the earth moves through its orbit, the Sun would appear to be moving against the backdrop of the fixed constellations, that is, from one zodiac sign to the other. The location of the Sun in any zodiac sign at the time of your birth is referred to as your Sun sign. In astronomical terms, this path of the Sun is known as the ecliptic, which is the apparent path traced by the Sun through the constellations of the zodiac, making a full circle in a year."

"You mean the Sun moves through the Zodiac? I thought the Sun was always at the same spot."

"Well, there is an apparent movement of the Sun against the Zodiac that we see as the earth moves around the Sun.

This is similar to the way a tree appears to move towards or away from you as you drive in a car. The same applies to not just the Sun, but also to other planets. They too appear to be moving through the Zodiac. The minute hand then represents this slower motion of the earth around the Sun, resulting in the planets and the Sun appearing to move through the twelve Zodiac signs."

"What about the hour hand then? What does that possibly represent?"

"Ah, that is a little bit more difficult to understand. It represents the movement referred to as the precession of equinoxes. The principles behind this motion require understanding a number of astronomical concepts like the inclination of the earth's axis, the celestial equator and the equinoxes."

"I am afraid what you just said went right over my head!"

"Well there is a simplified way to picture it in your mind. Assume that you mark the location of the Sun against the constellations of the zodiac today at this time, say 4pm exactly. Now let the earth make a full revolution around the Sun, letting a year pass. The next year, at the exact same date and time you mark the location of the Sun against the constellations again. You'll see that there is a very slight shift of the Sun from the position marked the previous year. The Sun would appear to have moved slightly against the fixed backdrop of the zodiac. And every year on the same date and time you can perceive this very gradual shift from the previous year, which accumulates over the years and results in the Sun appearing to cross over into another constellation or zodiac sign. It takes more than two thousand years for this apparent movement of the Sun from one zodiac sign to the other."

"So it is like the many rotations of the minute hand resulting in a gradual shifting of the hour hand?"

"You got it! By this notion, the Sun, or the vernal equinox to be precise, is currently in the constellation of Pisces. It will transition into the constellation of Aquarius by the end of the year 2012. That is, from the age of Pisces to the age of

Aquarius. By our analogy of the clock, it is then as though the solar clock strikes an hour at that time. And you know that many of our own appointments are usually on the hour or the half-hour!"

"There you go on about appointments again! What do you mean?"

"It is quite simple, Emma. We use the clock as a reference to order our personal life, such as a visit to the dentist, a business appointment, office times, a lunch break, whatever. These are appointments and schedules we make, by choice or otherwise, and we try to keep them. Likewise, there seem to be greater appointments and schedules of the soul that span a lifetime. These too seem to be ordered against a clock, a cosmic clock if you will, which is the solar system itself. What better choice exists than this great celestial clock-work that needs no springs or batteries, always keeps precise time, never stops but runs through the ages, and is visible to all who care to look? Its precision and durability are beyond our own watches and calendars."

Emma found this unnerving. "That sounds spooky, if you ask me! A clock out there in the sky! Appointments of the soul! I can't decide my own life then? There is no free will for me?"

"On the contrary! It is quite the same as all other appointments you make. You are free to make or break appointments, aren't you? But if you think about it, there are some appointments that you would not risk breaking, and there are those that you absolutely need to make, in your own interests. Your free will always allows you not to make or meet any such appointment, but the cost in some cases would probably be too dear. Peter is probably learning something of the sort right now!"

"Peter? Huh! So the planets don't drag fish like Peter into my life nor take them away. Isn't that what you are saying?"

"Well, not any more than the watch on your wrist does. Any influences or arrangements that seem to happen, apparently originate from the soul or the higher self, which recognizes that the time for an appointment is at hand."

"Soul arrangements, indeed! And what about the outcome of such appointments? Are those decided beforehand? Like for example, would Peter come calling again?"

"It is much the same as any other appointment you make, like a job interview. You can make an educated guess as to the outcome, also plan and prepare well for it so that a meeting has a good chance of being successful. Ultimately it is the free will of many individuals that decides the outcome. But when it comes to relationships, most of us do not often exercise our free will to change situations, do we? We are usually driven by our emotional natures. Then it is more or less easy to foresee what happens."

"But those soul appointments do take place, do they?"

"Not necessarily. Appointments can be canceled, re-scheduled, or entirely new appointments made. It seems to depend on a blueprint or plan for your life and how it has progressed so far. Astrology cannot say anything about changes to that schedule, other than give some broad indications – for the soul itself would not know the details beforehand."

"So there can be brilliant successes and total failures in predictions?"

"Predictions? I don't think the system is established for the purposes of predictions or fortune telling. It seems to be there to provide a rough idea about yourself, and the challenges and the goals that your soul or higher self has set for itself. In no case is the system in control, and you should not be looking to it for petty reasons."

"Okay, okay, but you said that it provides a rough idea about myself. How can a clock do anything like that? One of these books says that Virgo people are hypo-critical. How could such characteristics be imposed by a clock?"

"The answer again is that they can't. But let me explain by way of an analogy." Aliyah paused a moment, then continued. "Just this last week was the local kindergarten roundup, you know, when the school district tries to get all the local five-year-olds registered for kindergarten. Last Tuesday a friend of mine participated in the roundup, to register her little boy for school. I tagged along, curious to see what happened there. Her husband had instructed her to get to the school gym by 3 pm and we were there on the dot, followed the clock exactly. Guess what I found most interesting there?"

"I don't have any brats and you know I am not too fond of them either. But I expect you went there to gape at the kids," offered Emma.

"Well, I sure was interested in the kids and was listening to some of the registrations, and then it dawned on me that most of the kids being registered had last names starting with P, Q, R and S. It happened as a coincidence that I noticed, but then it took some time for me to figure it out. I asked some names randomly to make sure, and most names fell into this alphabet range. A few of them did not match though. One had a last name starting with Z, another had a V. However the overall correlation with the alphabet pattern was pretty strong! Now is that amazing or what?"

"Well, I don't think so!" laughed Emma. "They must have sent out a notice of some sort. Like specific appointment times based on the last name of the kids! Boy, aren't you gullible!"

Aliyah laughed too. "You're right! For a moment I was taken by surprise. In fact the school had circulated a flyer asking parents to preferably register kids according to a schedule. The schedule mapped the first alphabet in their last names to certain days and times. Well, all parents could not follow the guidelines as they had their own agendas and appointments that conflicted with these timings. And my friend hadn't seen the flyer, but simply did what her husband had instructed."

"All right! I see what you are getting at. You are comparing those kids' last names with astrological characteristics associated with birthdates and signs. And the school registration to birth itself."

"Yes! The characteristics and events described by astrology come about by arrangement, like my friend registering her boy for school. Those rules are not written in stone. Neither the planets nor the schools have any magical powers to enforce them."

"But that is not what popular interpretations of astrology seem to say. Some imply that planets send out some kind of waves or something and cause such things to happen."

"Well if you think about it, that line of reasoning is not completely invalid. You know that the moon causes tides, raising the water a few feet through the action of gravity. The land also rises, though it is less obvious. So the planets, at least those close to the earth, like Mercury, Venus, Mars and the Moon, can have some tangible effect on matter, even the brain. But translating that to what is popularly claimed about astrology is a singular stretch of the imagination."

"You mean the contentions of astrologers have no basis?"

"Look at it again, Emma. Planetary positions or movements that are used in astrology are in most cases only appearances. They are virtual positions and movements, not real. The Sun does not actually move through the Zodiac in such a fashion. It is only an appearance, much like a tree appearing to move when you drive your car. It would be ridiculous to say that your moving tree hit a pedestrian, or that the "conjunction" of the tree with the pedestrian had a physical impact. Whereas in fact the tree remained where it is, the pedestrian was not close to the tree, and they did not even interact. It is only in your view from the car that they seemed to have come together. How can something virtual or illusory cause a real physical effect?"

"All right then, let's suppose that you are right. And let's even suppose that this thing does work by arrangement, and that this solar clock drives this arrangement. But you have pushed back the problem. Where did this solar clock come from?"

"Indeed, Emma, that is the biggest question. There is the problem of the origin of this solar clock and why the clock would even be consulted at all. Apparently there is a greater order to life that spans though the ages, and there seems to be plans, purposes and deadlines as well, for otherwise a clock is not needed. If you notice, the solar clock can tell time from hours to the great ages, that is, from small durations to years, to a lifetime, and then again to even greater spans of time if you consider the precession of the equinoxes. This means there are plans, purposes and deadlines at the level of individuals, nations, and even for the race itself!"

"Whoa, hold on! That's stretching things far too much!"

"But Emma, why else would a clock tell time across the ages, unless the human race as a whole has plans, purposes and deadlines that span ages? Just think of that! A clock that strikes for the human race as a whole, as if the race were a single individual!"

"Aliyah, you are boggling the mind now. This is pretty hard to digest. Plans and purposes for the human race? How can there be any? Where can they come from?"

"Where can they come from? There is a hint, if you look carefully. Before batteries came along, you were the one who wound up your clock or watch, providing the energy that makes it tick, so that you could order your life. Now consider this great solar clock-work. What is it that created and continues to drive it?"

"The Sun, I should think."

"And what does the Sun stand for in our analogies?"

"*Your* analogies, you mean. Yes, in your analogies it seems to correspond to, what do you call it… the Godhead?"

"Well, religious people do attribute plans and purposes in life to a higher source, don't they? And isn't it curious how we keep coming back to this notion of the Sun as an analogue of the Godhead?"

Emma pondered this. It seemed that Aliyah's system of inquiry consistently pointed out this analogy with the Sun. Was there really a greater order to life as these analogies seemed to hint?

"So you have concluded from your research that astrology is true? That all you have said has a firm basis? Then why do astrologers come out with conflicting predictions and analysis all the time?"

"Hmm, yes, good question. Now how shall I put this?" Aliyah looked down and pondered a while. Then she smiled and looked up.

"Remember the time you told me that Jen had eloped with one of your science instructors? And you were really buzzing all over about it?"

"Sure, I remember," Emma grinned sheepishly.

"There was even speculation that the fellow had taken all of his wife's jewels with him. But in truth Jen had simply left without notice to attend her grandmother's funeral, and all your instructor had done was give her a lift to the airport."

"That was not my fault at all! I got that bit of news from what I thought was quite a reliable source, but it turned out that she didn't get all of it quite right." Emma flushed a crimson red.

"Indeed," laughed Aliyah. "Such is the very nature of gossip. Information is relayed from one person to another through individual descriptions of what each has understood. Gossip spreads, mutates, combines and regenerates in many forms. What you or I might hear would usually be a caricature of the actual thing or event. So you can think of so many variants of the same information available to different people, distorted, some even absolutely false. This invariably happens when information is relayed through many people."

"I see what you are getting at. You are saying that the astrological system of interpretation has mutated into many forms, the way gossip does?"

"Yes, primarily because the system has been relayed through generations of people who have followed what was handed down, then embellished or distorted it in some way and passed it on, in many cases orally. The truer interpretations are now esoteric and rarely to be found. But many systems are acceptable approximations. At the same time, many others are also far from it. The current state of affairs is really no reason to throw the baby out with the bath water."

"And what is a true system of interpretation, if I may ask?"

"Well, I believe that the closer a system is to the right interpretation, the more focus it will give on your soul, its plans and purposes, its goals and failures, its challenges. The farther away a system is, the more it will focus on petty things like whether you will find romance this week, make a pile at the stock market, or get a promotion – which will appear to work brilliantly or fail miserably by virtue of simple statistics. But what is more important, a true system will always focus on the real reasons behind the trials you face and why you have made certain goals for yourself. For you see, without meaning and reason, any plan or purpose is lost."

"Are you saying that astrology is not really meant for predictions?"

"That is right! It is not meant to be used for predictions any more than a clock or calendar is. I can always try to predict by looking at your calendar that next month you will have a surgical appointment. Maybe you will, or maybe it will be postponed or cancelled. What is the point? The information one would seek is really as to why you have that appointment and how you might be able to avoid surgery or at least prepare for it. Such is the information provided by a true astrological interpretation, which is written against your soul calendar."

Emma felt dizzy. All of this was too much information to digest. It seemed that in a single line of reasoning Aliyah had moved from her watch to the solar system and from it to a greater order.

Suddenly her watch buzzed and she looked at it quizzically. It would soon be twelve noon.

"There's one appointment for me now! But that reminds me. What do you think will happen in 2012?"

"Nothing, really." replied Aliyah.

"Nothing? But you said it's time for some appointment for the race or something?"

"Well, don't expect anything magical in that year! It is like any of our appointments. At the start of an appointment there is the preparation of entering into some activity. Like when you visit the dentist you go through the process of registering, waiting, going in, settling down, idle chit-chat, while things are being prepared and questions are being asked. Or when you meet for lunch you sit down, look through the menu, order items, make idle talk. And it takes a while before the actual activity commences. Astrologers are aware of this equivalent phenomenon."

"Equivalent phenomenon?"

"It takes about a few degrees of rotation of the clock hand, a mark of time, until the influence of a previous zodiac sign wanes and the current sign becomes fully prominent. So this means you can expect perhaps a few hundred years or so to go by before the race as a whole fully sees and recognizes that something major has happened. Individuals of course may possibly recognize it much earlier."

"Well, whatever. I really must leave now. Mom will be waiting at the mall. And she really gets hopping mad if I don't show up on time. Isn't that just finicky?"

As she drove, Emma couldn't help glancing at her watch time and again. Aliyah's cosmic clock kept coming back to her mind. Was it possible that the cosmos somehow had an intelligent watch maker?

Holidays came and went. Aliyah eagerly looked forward to seeing Theo again after the break. On the first day of school, she walked quickly to the hall where Theo would be offering his new course. Outside the lecture hall there was a small crowd. She could hear loud conversations and exclamations among the group of students. Something was going on.

"What's up?" she asked a colleague.

"The course was cancelled! They don't have anyone capable of handling it."

"I thought Prof. Thor was pretty good with it." She felt tension rise within.

"Oh, you didn't hear the news? Everyone's talking about him!"

"News? what news?" A cold dread of fear slipped into her.

"The guy was some sort of adventurer; worked for the secret service too. They say he went on a mission to South America, chasing drug runners."

"And?" she questioned anxiously. The description was familiar.

"The last they heard, there was some contract out on him. They tried to help him out of the country, but…"

"But?"

"He never got out alive, the poor chap. Guess those fellows over there are really vicious."

She hardly heard the rest. Her knees felt weak and her vision turned hazy. Voices around became a rumble and she leaned against the wall to support herself. The earth shook, thunder clapped and the sky came crashing down. Theo had disappeared from her life.

In the days that followed, Aliyah moved around in stunned silence and pain, questioning herself how such a thing could ever happen. All her efforts to meditate were futile. It seemed there was nothing she could do to end her pain. She was amazed at herself, that all her spiritual practices and her so-called wisdom were easily negated by down-to-earth human experiences and emotions. And she could do nothing about it. How could anyone be free and enlightened, she wondered, when the onslaught of basic human emotion was so fundamental and overpowering? For the hundredth time she asked herself if there were at all any meaning or purpose to life.

But life never gave her answers in speeches or in letters, for her truths were always meant to be forged within her own being.

And to get there, she had to first fall victim to abject and diabolical evil.

8. Web

Aliyah recognizes various levels of evil, reflected in the habitat of a spider.

The spider had spun its gossamer web in a long series of agile movements. The web was built in a large orb that started from its outer edges, spiraling all the way to the center and terminating in a small networked platform, the hub, where the spider lurked, waiting for its prey. It knew by instinct that flies and insects frequented this location. The stench of rotting food and other wastes from the city drains were strong and attracted many denizens of the insect world into these dark alleys. Like the dark forces signified by its pattern, the spider was large, scary and loathsome in appearance. It avoided the light and preferred dark or shaded corners, and usually hunted in the night. Its eight dark and spiny legs and its eight eyes signified the dark ones' allegiance to the forces of retribution. For the number eight represented the forces of reaction to action, of sowing and reaping, of that which caused the results of an action to ultimately impinge back, returning to the agent of causation. Even the shape of the numeral was comprised of two returning arcs or circles, the higher one signifying the return of good, and the lower one that of evil. The spider's body itself had the same figure of-eight, with the lower circle often greatly emphasized.

And the spiral that started at the periphery of the web terminated at the spider, representing the downward spiral of spiritual degeneration that ended in utter destruction, the vital essences of a trapped and degenerated soul being ultimately absorbed into the dark ones, just as the spider sucked out the juices of its prey. In the successful hunter's web was to be found the shriveled bodies of various insects, which ultimately fell down to the ground and decomposed into the body of the earth, for the spider's mouth parts could not take in solid food but only the vital liquids of its prey. The dark ones too preyed on the vital energies of a trapped soul, and the soul stuff drained of all its organizing and sustaining energies was left to decompose away into the body of God. It took the light of spiritual discernment to recognize their complex webs of deceit, just as it took the glint of sunlight to reveal a spider web. The web itself, sticky, intricate, invisible and hovering in air, represented patterns of thoughts and emotions abetted and encouraged by the dark ones. These patterns compelled souls to indulge in certain activities which, when carried further, dragged them into an ever-accelerating downward spiral of destruction. The dark ones were exceedingly crafty and clever, and adept at spinning elaborate, complex and invisible patterns of deceit.

And the spider waited motionlessly in its web with infinite patience, as though it knew that its prey would surely come.

Aliyah had entered this South American country on a mission of personal importance. Paramount were her memories of Theo and the legacy he had left behind. The other was her association with a number of social welfare groups working with children and teenagers who were in need of counseling and support. Too often she had witnessed the literal devastation that resulted from the abuse of narcotic drugs, and such a pitiful wasting away of young lives had evoked both a deep compassion and a righteous anger within her. Combined with her feelings for Theo and the cause for his death, they had created in her a personal vendetta.

Her meticulous research on the trafficking and distribution of certain drugs had led her to a study of some major supply chains that originated in some countries in the tropics. As a social worker with a reputed multi-national organization, she had asked for, nay, demanded, that she be assigned to a special project. A project where she could get an opportunity to personally investigate drug abuse and its criminal origins, in a country she was determined to enter at any cost. This was quite a dangerous motive but none could dissuade her from following it through. Her decision also came from a simple guilelessness and a foolish innocence that often bestowed a kind of courage on her, creating a drive to explore grounds that others feared to tread.

The country was unlike anything she had seen before. Much of its population was poor, and yet there was blatant opulence displayed by those in power. The drug cartels ruled the country with their shadowy hands, like puppet masters. They had penetrated all aspects of government, from the legislature and the judiciary to the police and military forces. Even the churches and the news media were not left untouched. With billions of dollars being generated from the trafficking business and a population poor enough to cater to the trafficker's demands, the drug lords and their hierarchies of henchmen had the country fully in their grip. And they maintained it by systematically bribing or destroying opposition, and resorting to violence and bloodshed, including mass murder. Even the highest office in the country was supposedly on their payroll and any who dared voice dissent or refused to cooperate were destroyed mercilessly.

There was little she could do in terms of exposing the political nexus with the mafia, for this was common knowledge among the populace. Her intent was to generate sufficient documentation that could highly escalate the perceived threat level originating from such countries. This, with sufficient lobbying, could help aggravate the foreign policies of various nations of the world toward these countries, forcing the political system to react and shake off the deeply entrenched tentacles of the drug mafia. But to do this she needed facts and statistics on drug volumes, the labor force, chemical plants, air fields, destinations, distribution networks and so on. And these she hoped to amass from field work and from interviewing various people at all levels, from peasants to politicians.

Surprisingly, the peasants were willing to talk and most of them seemed to support the drug cartels. Their cultivation and sale of their crops provided them with much higher profits than they could hope to gain otherwise. The drug lords had even pumped some of the money into social welfare programmes, such as constructing houses, building roads, and disbursing grants. All these gave them a veneer of legitimacy and they were seen by many as great benefactors. The disastrous effects of their trade, their penchant for violence and bloodshed, and their system of corruption and control were often overlooked.

While people in the labor force were willing to provide information, often based on gossip, those at higher levels offered little help and resisted all her attempts. And her colleagues in the news media always warned her of danger, for they had been persecuted too often for their efforts and many of their people had been murdered for going against the will of the mafia. The drug lords had a system of issuing contracts on targets that hit-men or bounty hunters would take up in hope of collecting huge rewards. The contracts were often aimed at specific individuals among politicians, judges, newspaper editors, lawyers and so on, but at times they also targeted generic classes of officials such as the police. In such instances, rewards were offered by head count, making each and every member of the institution valid prey, with deadly consequences. Thus the drug lords had achieved total control of the system. There was little hope that Aliyah could achieve anything.

But to her surprise, she was able to make good progress with her research. It seemed that the system was so sure of itself with its threats of elimination that it looked upon her with amusement, as if in a game of cat and mouse. Through the peasants she could establish contacts into the higher pyramid of the labor force, visit their habitations and collect samples and gather statistics. She made sure that her questions and inquiries were not the probing kind, and instead chose to listen to what each level was willing to divulge. She could always find higher-level people in the labor force who could discuss what they did for a living, for it was often the case that people knew only of their own local operations and had no complete picture of the larger system. And she took discreet photographs whenever she could.

After months of research, she started analyzing her information, mapping the points onto one another, looking for consistency. And to her delight a pattern began to emerge. She knew her statistics were based mostly on what she had heard people talk about, but taken together from various strata of the labor force and across geographical regions, much of her information was generally consistent. The numbers began to make sense as she constructed layered pyramids out of her statistics, with each pyramid under an individual drug lord. Various strata of the labor force were segmented across these pyramids, but there was also considerable overlap at the bases where peasants did not seem to be too concerned about who they sold their crop to. And there was some kind of cooperation between the drug lords as well, for many distribution chains were often used by all of them.

Then she compiled all the numbers into a single chart, and noticed that she could use a better structure than a typical organizational pyramid. For one, the top portion of the pyramid that handled processing, distribution and exercised control over the system was much too small compared to that of the peasant labor force. But most importantly, the peasants were not really an integral part of the mafia, though the mafia made use of them. And there were no useful pyramidal structures within the peasant population. There were limited interactions between the two, like transfer of goods and money and some control. The peasant work force existed as an almost independent unit, functionally separate, but subservient to the mafia's control and coordination machinery. Therefore Aliyah decided to segregate the functional mafia from the peasants as two separate entities. She represented these two factions as two self-contained ovals joined together, a smaller one on top interfacing with and controlling a larger one at the bottom. And from the top oval sprang the distribution channels, a channel of movement for drugs, reaching out to other countries of the world. She drew them as thick lines emanating from the small oval, and all of a sudden the caricature of a spider was staring back at her from the drawing sheet!

This image struck her so hard that she paused, wondering at the correlation. For one, were a spider's legs, really all of them, attached to the cephalothorax or the small oval? All it took for confirmation was to walk over to a corner of the room where she could inspect a spider in its web. Now back at her table, she stared hard at the drawing, brows furrowed. Was her imagination running too wild?

She could easily complete the picture with a web, for the first level distribution chains expanded into a proper web that spanned a large number of countries. This was the sticky part of the web that trapped millions of innocents and consumed them. There was also another network at the center of the web, one that handled production and exercised local control. This was quite like the central hub network of the web where the spider lurked waiting for its prey. The mouthparts of the spider, its brains, the numerous eyes, the poison glands and the venom-injecting claws she could easily associate with the small oval. The large oval of the peasants represented the abdomen that processed and generated all the energy required for the sustenance of this spider. Moreover, the silk glands of the spider were located in the abdomen, and it was this silk that was spun by the spider using its legs to weave the gossamer webs that trapped its victims. Likewise it was the peasant labor force represented by the larger oval that produced the drug crop, which was then processed and distributed by the mafia into the web. A further revealing fact was that the rudimentary heart of the spider, a simple tube, was located not in the cephalothorax or the small oval, but rather in the abdomen. The small oval of the spider representing the mafia was literally heartless! The correlation was particularly striking, and it strongly hinted that perhaps there was a real connection between the patterns of a spider and that of the drug mafia. She then remembered that most spiders were cannibalistic by nature and would destroy members of their own species when they could. Such was true of the mafia as well, for they tended to separate into rival factions and kill off one another in bitter contests for power and territory. Occasionally they would cooperate when circumstances favored, but in general they were quite wary of one another, like most spiders. Her picture of a spider in a web in a tropical jungle now represented a greater pattern that existed on a much larger scale!

Things seemed to be going well, with her research about to bear fruit, when all of a sudden her world was turned upside down. She had made a crucial mistake in confiding the contents of her dossier to a friend in the police. The dossier she had compiled was now quite large, with photographs and also statistics on production rates, labor force strata, distribution channels and resources, and estimates of drug volumes moving out of the country, among others. With these numbers she could also work out the amount of land under cultivation to sustain outflow rates. Large masses of land literally under the very noses of various governmental programmes had to be used in the production of these drugs, and this was an additional compelling factor to champion her cause. But it seemed too late, for the news of her research leaked and the top bosses were angry. Then word came that a mafia contract was out on her and if she wanted to live, she had better get out quickly. She found herself running, and running scared, afraid even to ask the local authorities for protection, for she suspected that she would not be the least bit safe with them. She had received anonymous phone calls and messages that confirmed and reiterated threats of death.

She ran through the dark alley, panting and gasping, desperately looking for some place of refuge. Her pursuers were closing in and they probably knew this place very well. There was the sound of a shot being fired. A bullet whizzed past her head as she made a turn into an alley. Frantically, she kept running, turning into various alleys, as her pursuers gradually narrowed in on her. Then she stumbled and turned again into yet another alley, one that was darker than most others. But running a bit further ahead, she was in for a shock. She had suddenly reached a dead-end, with no way forward or up. To go back would be certain death, for she could hear the sound of running footsteps. She cringed into a dark corner, her body pressed against the walls, mind almost numb in terror as she desperately tried to think of a way out. It was hopeless and there was nothing she could do to save herself from disaster. She knew that her assailants would show no mercy and no bargains could be made.

And in that crazed moment of terror something strange took hold of her being and dragged her memories back into a long forgotten period of her childhood. The image of herself as an innocent child, with her childishly simple prayers in the face of hardship, now became prominent. This trust in providence and belief in prayer had once been an active part of her being and now it struggled to express itself again. Having no other choice and yielding to that strange calling within, she found herself invoking the Lord's name. His prayer, words she had banished from her mind for so long, now forcefully entered her awareness. Perhaps the prayer was a desperate last hope. Perhaps it came from the faint remembrance of sober advice from an aged soldier who had said of that prayer, "In the face of abject evil, do not panic. Hold off your fear at all costs and say the Lord's Prayer. It has tremendous power to shield you from evil."

She sobbed, bit her trembling lips and recited the Lord's Prayer, again and again. Shouts came from nearby and she heard footsteps coming closer. A beam from a flashlight lit through the alley, scanning the walls, looking for her. The beam went over her body and she was sure that they had seen her. The beam flickered and went out and came on again. For a brief moment, it illuminated a large web next to her head. The spider scurried away as the beam moved on. Eyes closed and jaw set tight, she held her breath and braced herself for the impact of a bullet. None came, for the beam went off and she soon heard receding footsteps. Her pursuers were looking for her in another direction. All of a sudden, there came distant shouts and the sound of gunfire. In the semi-darkness she could see one of her assailants fall as the others returned fire. A fight ensued, and bullets hailed back and forth through the alleys. She saw dark figures running, the sound of their footsteps receding fast. Her pursuers seemed to have taken off, having lost all interest in her. What was going on? Soon a heavy silence descended and she dropped to her knees, sobbing pitifully. She couldn't believe they hadn't seen her. She was still alive, by sheer luck or a miracle.

Aliyah staggered out of the alley into the open, tears streaming down her cheeks. In a daze, and knees shaking, she hardly knew which way to go. But as soon as she took a few shaky steps forward, a dark figure appeared from the shadows and moved quickly towards her. Seeing the dark apparition appear from nowhere, she started to scream, but the figure quickly grabbed her by the waist and clamped a hand over her mouth.

"Hush!" came the gruff voice of a man. "They could still be around."

With effort, she contained her panic and then nodded her head, eyes wide. The figure studied her for a moment and then released her gently. She tried to walk forward but found herself stumbling, for she was still recovering from shock.

"We have to move quickly. Let me help you." The man approached her and in a quick motion swept her off her feet and into his arms. She found herself being carried through the darkness and tried to resist. Finding it fruitless, she gave up and turned her attention to studying this stranger who now carried her effortlessly, as if she were a kitten. But she could not make out anything in the darkness, for a black cloth covered his face and also muffled his voice.

The stranger moved quickly and silently among the dark shadows, pausing every now and then to listen to the silence and to look back on his trail. He seemed tense but moved with cat-like agility. Soon she could see that he was heading for a wide street that faced the alley, well lit and with people about.

She suddenly found herself on her feet again. The stranger thrust something into her palm.

"Here," he said, "keys to that small black car you see next to the street light. Get over to the airport now, and fast! You will find your papers and an air ticket in the back seat. Do not stop for anything or anyone, not even for the police. Now move; we are running short of time!"

"Who are you?" she asked. "And why do you help me?"

"That doesn't matter. You must get out now! Go!"

"But what about you?" she enquired, still dizzy.

"I can take care of myself. Now get the hell out of here!"

He sounded angry and very concerned.

Aliyah trudged towards the car and opened the door. She turned back to look down the alley. She could faintly see the stranger lurking in the shadows, watching her. She waved to him, got into the car and tried the keys. The engine quickly purred to life.

Back on a plane to her home country, Aliyah finally breathed a sigh of relief. Her escape was almost miraculous. Was it her prayer that had saved her? How did that man come to be there at that time? Who was he? She remembered that she never got to thank him, and now she never would.

Her thoughts quickly drifted to Theo. She now had the satisfaction of having completed what he had begun. She would see to it that his work was not wasted. Her personal vendetta would be fulfilled.

She picked up her dossier and leafed through it, again going through all the material she had collected. The data was prime for reporting and she needed to think and analyze how she would present it to the public. Turning another page, her eyes fell upon the caricature of the spider that she had drawn. Gazing at it, she felt there was more to the issue than was obvious so far and decided to step back and look at the whole picture afresh. Perhaps she would find further insights into the mafia that she could use.

The very notion that such a system could exist and in close proximity to democratic nations of the world was a major surprise. Akin to the contrasting physical terrains that existed side by side on the earth, here was an instance of contrasting terrains existing close together in human minds, at the scale of societies and even nations. Were they reflections of each other? Her system of analogies did predict such an outcome. She had discovered that the spiderweb as a physical pattern was also an analogy of a similar pattern that existed in humans, such as that evinced by the drug mafia. Why spiders alone? Indeed many species that surrounded man could then be reflections of his nature. The gentleness of a doe, the relentlessness of a badger, the deadly traps of a spider or the killing venom of a snake, all represented human natures too in various ways. They seemed proper reflections of man's nature, especially those species with which man was most familiar. The native Americans, who had a tradition of respecting and treating the earth as holy ground, and who had long observed her patterns, had maintained that each man resembled some animal by his nature.

But the similarity seemed to extend into the very anatomies of these species, if her spider analogy were correct, as though individual people were like cells that formed various organs within a larger animal body. A kind of super-organism built up from groups of like people that functioned like various organs, with each group having specific tasks and natures. A body seemed to be built, in the case of the mafia, based on organizing principles that were to be found reflected in the anatomy of a spider. Could it also be possible that there existed other such super-organisms in the world, organized around patterns which were also reflected in other species?

She tried extending her correlations to societies, cultures, nations and geographic locations of the earth, against species that were to be found there. The hot tropical areas of the earth, indeed, were generally infested with insects, snakes and various other species classified as vermin. These areas were also where one usually found a rampant display of turbulent and heated emotions and their resulting actions, and also a graphic portrayal of the pathos of life. The temperate regions generally hosted species that were more moderate in nature, and most of the so-called developed nations of today were to be found in those regions. It was also a curious fact that many nations had some animal motif associated with them, such as the Russian bear, the American eagle, or the Chinese dragon. While this did not expressly imply that these nations had any of those characteristics, the fact that such associations existed meant something. There seemed to be some level of meaning to her correlations.

Did the pattern of the spider have an analogue at even higher levels? The system she had left behind was indeed a complete hierarchy of powers and policies, but aligned to principles of greed and fear. Her system of correlations now pointed to the existence of a similar system of evil at the level of the spirit, one to which she had hardly attributed such complexity and organizational skills. She was familiar with the notion of demonic forces and had even been psychically attacked a few times, but she had not suspected that there could be such large and rigorously organized bodies of evil at the level of the spirit, hierarchically structured and aligned to dark principles of greed, fear and separation. If they did exist, what was their role in the scheme of things?

The spider now presented itself as a clue. These dark legions of the spirit were natural outcomes of a higher evolution, a spiritual species that chose to evolve into a predatory mode of life. Like the spiders that controlled insect populations in an ecosystem, they too had a role in the evolution of the human spirit, that of identifying and eliminating the vermin within man, those given irredeemably to darker instincts. Many such as were found swelled the ranks of these legions, aligned to dark principles that sought selfish interests. But this did not mean that they were irredeemable, for strong insects could tear off a spider's web with effort and gain their freedom, and one rarely found butterflies caught in spiders' webs, due to evolutionary adaptations of their wings. Even the spider's area of influence was limited and contained. There were no six-foot spiders lurking in the neighborhood, preying on unsuspected humans or larger animals. Still, spiders were to be found almost everywhere, from remote jungles to corporate boardrooms. Here was another reflection of the pattern, for it meant that the dark ones had entrenched themselves into virtually all institutions and habitats of man. Their invisible webs of deceit were to be found spanning all aspects of human life.

Could the world stop drug trafficking at all? She knew it was very difficult, for species thrived on the availability of food, and as long as consumer nations harbored the tendencies that made them seek narcotic drugs, as long as the heavy demand existed, the trafficking would continue. Controlling the supply chain of drugs was one method of partially addressing the problem, but that was not the solution. The solution had to ultimately arise from the consumer side, and those who sought these drugs needed to control and cleanse themselves. The solution was not to be found in the destruction of spiders, but in the cleansing of one's habitation so that insects were no longer dragged in, followed by spiders.

Again she found herself reciting the Lord's Prayer. She did not resist it but let the words flow out from her soul. And with a mysterious peace within her heart, she slept.

Somewhere else in the scheme of things a dark force gingerly tested its web of deceit, and found some strands broken. A contract had terminated, above and below.

Her adventure into the higher realms of the day side[2] had begun.

<hr />

[2] See chapter 'Sky'

9. Tree of Life

Aliyah connects with her higher self and finds its analogy in nature.

Fire rose up from the earth and ran up her spine, sprouting branches like a pine tree. The fire gave of itself to innumerable leaves, the energy vortices that were constantly at work within her inner tree. The leaves required this contribution from the earth to make use of the heavenly light from the great source above. That supernal light from on high always split into a rainbow of colors, with seven primary colors and innumerable intermediate shades of colors as they continuously bathed her tree in its radiance.[3]

The rising fire energized seven main branches and innumerable minor branches of her inner tree, helping the

---

[3] See 'kundalini' in glossary

leaves to absorb and process the flood of heavenly light into her personality. This contribution received from the earth, the life force from the air[4] and the light from on high, helped build, sustain and nourish her higher bodies, their delicate tissues.[5] She was quite unaware of such a metabolism of higher life that was active within everything that was alive. The fire from the earth usually did not make its presence felt, but was often a flickering flame in many. In them it only energized certain pathways as it could, for many pathways were blocked, atrophied or corrupted. This created an imbalance within the personality, like a tree that had twisted itself into an odd shape, with some branches much thicker than others, some atrophied, and unable to grow in symmetry. The light could not properly nourish a tree when it was diseased, riven with parasites, or blocked out from the light by the presence of other trees that kept it in shade.

But as she danced and sang to the Lord, the fire from the earth literally forced itself into all the branches and pathways, rising higher into the domains of the subtle and higher frequencies, where it met an incoming flood of higher light. There it worked a secret alchemy within her consciousness, a complex light or photosynthesis that often transported her into indescribable, psychedelic and blissful states of consciousness accompanied by visions and prophetic symbolism. Rarely was she aware of the fire rising within, for many of her pathways were pure like those of a child and the fire met little resistance. But today she was particularly conscious of its fiery nature as it rose and transported her into a state of bliss beyond description, a mode of consciousness where heaven met the earth and she was one with all that she experienced. Her personality had temporarily submerged back into soul consciousness, where she was allowed a fleeting glimpse into her own greater reality. The tree had experienced its oneness with the earth as she submerged for a while into an aspect of the manifested

---

[4] See 'prana' in glossary
[5] Compare with the role of sunlight, water and minerals within a natural tree

Godhead. The sun was shining and the Lord was above all the earth, smiling down on her.

"See that tree, Emma? That's me! See that cloud? That's me! And look at you! I am you!" She danced and sang in ecstasy.

"You're crazy!" laughed Emma. "Are you on drugs or something?"

"No, no!" cried Aliyah as she strove to contain her bliss, her face set in a big grin which was the best she could do to show some apparent normalcy of behavior. "It's all grace from the Lord! He is everywhere and in everything! Look what He's done today!"

It took about an hour for her to get back to normal. Emma was watching, fascinated, though quite skeptical of what was going on. Aliyah sighed, relaxed back into a chair and looked at Emma with eyes of love. She wished there were some way she could convey the logic of it all, and she pondered a while before speaking.

"Emma, I know it is hard to understand. But remember our system of analogies, particularly that of the solar system? I think there is a proper explanation to be found there."

Indeed there was. The solar system with its void of space, the Sun and the planets, represented the Godhead with its aspects of the Great Void, The Creator and the Manifested God.[6] The Earth thus represented God manifest, or the body of God, from which originated all life. The trees, plants and grasses that rose from the earth under the life-giving rays of the Sun represented life-streams that originated from the body of God, energized by the Creator, and in turn grew towards Him. The branching of a tree signified the branching of a life-stream, such as that of the human life-stream, where the life essences separated and segregated. A collection of leaves stemming from any terminal branch represented a manifested personality with its many facets and attributes, sent forth from the soul or higher self, represented by the stem of the branch. The other intermediate branches encountered as one traversed

---

[6] See chapter 'Dust'

the tree from a terminal branch to the ground represented soul structures above the higher self, as they progressively joined together to form one single tree rooted in the body of God. The trunk that rose from the ground thus represented the collective consciousness of the life-stream itself, which was in turn rooted into the consciousness of the manifested Godhead.

All leaves were connected with one another through the tree, but they formed preferential groupings such as branches and sub-branches that formed individual clusters of leaves. These preferential groupings within a life-stream represented souls and personalities as they manifested in national, social, racial and family contexts. Yet all humanity was connected in the great tree of life, and was literally one. No leaf or branch could hope to grow much higher than other leaves or branches, for its progress would ultimately be inhibited by the necessity of contributing to the progress of the rest of the tree, that of the welfare of its brethren. No branch or leaf was an isolated entity that progressed or regressed on its own, for its actions affected not only itself, but the whole tree as well.

And it was no accident that certain spiritual traditions compared souls to the branches of a tree or a vine. Like the leaves to a branch and the tree, a personality existing on the earth was fundamental to the growth and evolution of the spirit in man, and also to the human life-stream as a whole. The personality weathered earthly life, through which it processed its experiences of body, mind, emotions and spirit. These were reflected[7] in the function of the leaves as they worked with minerals, air, water and sunlight, preparing food in the form of sugars. Like the leaves that moved the food they processed into the branches, the personality transmitted its assimilated experience or learning to its own mother branch, the soul or higher self, and the learning percolated down and throughout the whole of the tree, contributing to overall growth.

---

[7] See chapter 'Desert'

"Are you saying that a single leaf represents a person, or is it a collection of leaves on a branch?" asked Emma.

"It could be either way, as long as one considers a branch, or specifically the stem of the branch holding the leaves, as representing the soul or higher self. Unlike the leaves, the stem has the same physiology as the rest of the tree. The higher self is also likewise, as it shares much in common with deeper levels of consciousness that exist in the human life-stream. There are, of course, unhealthy branches, those penetrated by parasites, hollowed out by insects or infected by disease-causing agents. These too represent the state of affairs within our tree of life."

"So where does your experience fit into this?"

"Well, it's not difficult to understand if you look at a growing branch, for instance. There you see an ongoing progression of growth. The branch keeps sprouting new buds that slowly grow into new leaves. Now this represents a progressive manifestation, an unfolding of capabilities, talents, nature, attributes and so on, funneled from the higher self into the personality. But then, some buds do not grow well, some atrophy, some are eaten by pests, some die. The same applies to various characteristics contributed from the higher self. But the ongoing growth, nevertheless, continues. This can go on for quite some time, allowing the leaves to process and store sufficient energy and food before the branch makes practically a quantum leap forward. Do you know what that is?"

"You mean that the branch flowers, don't you?"

"Yes! Flowering often starts as an induction or signal originating from the leaves, which is then passed on to the stem of the branch. Only when the leaves are ready and able to create this floral induction can flowering happen. The stem now responds by forming a floral bud instead of a leaf bud, which now grows and opens into a beautiful bloom, a literal precipitation of the life essence within the branch into a form one can perceive. A condensation of its very spiritual nature, if you will."

"I see, so your spiritual experiences are like the flowering of a tree or a plant?"

"Like the flowering of a branch, yes. Or even a tree, if one compares a personality to a tree rooted in the higher self, which is but another analogy. Our spiritual flowering is a manifestation of the God-spirit within, as it pours out into the consciousness of the personality. It is an indication of what the soul has made of itself, its best and purified essence, over its long period of evolution. In function and appearance a flower is vastly different from the leaves, don't you think?"

"Mmm. Yes. Flowers are quite different from the rest of the comparatively dull and weather-beaten tree. You are saying it represents spirituality."

"Well, it represents what one has made of one's God-stuff within. Everyone is unique in that sense, for a huge variety of flowers exist. You see, our analogy of a tree can also be extended to an ecosystem, such as a forest. The plants, grasses, shrubs, trees, all are representations of both individuals and life-streams. And there are plants that prey on others, those that trap insects, and there are also flowers that stink. These also represent what those life-streams or souls have made of their own god-stuff within."

"Is flowering related to your concept of enlightenment?"

"Call it a spiritual birth, for that is a better term. Each one has a unique experience of what it is like, simply because of one's evolutionary history. There are probably as many different experiences of the spiritual birth or enlightenment as there are people. Of course, there will be a lot of similar ground as well."

"How does one get to flower then? Is it something I can bring on by myself?"

"I must say, the matter is quite complex. The flowering process in plants and trees is still not fully understood. There are many factors affecting floral development across species. Many need to go through a long period of cold weather; some are sensitive to the length or duration of daylight, meaning specific phases during the earth's motion around the Sun. For most trees, age and development matters a lot, and the leaves must have accumulated sufficient energy to support floral development. There are also the desert plants that bloom incredibly quickly after a life-giving shower of rain from above. I suppose the analogies to human lives are understandable from these. In any case, the decision and the resulting outpouring of spirit comes from above. It is not in my or your control. But also note that a tree is genetically destined to flower."

"Very interesting. However, one fact conflicts with your analogy. Leaves die, fall to the ground and disintegrate, but that's not true when you consider souls or personalities, is it?"

"Ah, but that analogy is also true! You see, the human personality is composed not only of the consciousness and attributes projected by the higher self, but also incorporates a bodily consciousness and lower mind amalgamated by the very organization of the body. Before a leaf dies, its branch extracts out most of the sugar the leaf has prepared and then withdraws its sap from the leaf. Subsequently the leaf withers and falls to the earth to decompose into the soil. Similarly the higher self completes assimilation of the personality's learning and withdraws its life-essences. The body starts to disintegrate and the integrated bodily consciousness and its associated lower mind dissipate, back into the body of God. You can see that the analogy still holds."

"Hmm. What about the colors of autumn before a leaf dies? Do they signify anything?"

"Yes, the seasons have their story to tell as well. Personalities, souls, life streams, even the Godhead, all go through cyclic periods of birthing, expansive growth and exploration, followed by a period of application of what has been learnt, and finally a period of rest or return. These correspond to the seasons of the spring, summer, fall and winter. Then the cycle begins again. Our own life as it progresses from birth and childhood, schooling and vocational training, the taking up of a job where one is in service to one's nation, and then merging into the finale of death, holds a reflection of the seasons. Likewise, the human race or the life-stream as a whole also has its seasons."

"What's that got to do with the colors of the fall?"

"Well, let's look at what happens across the seasons. During summer, the leaves are highly active in preparing food and contributing to the growth process of the tree. But later in autumn, a period sets in when all such activity wanes. Now instead of showing the color green, the true colors of the leaves start to manifest. The green coloring was due to the overwhelming presence of chlorophyll, a necessity for proc essing food. It swamped out all other pigments present in the leaves." Aliyah paused.

"Then what happens?"

"Now this green chlorophyll is withdrawn, allowing other pigments present within the leaves to show through. Not only that, all the sugar generated by a leaf is not withdrawn into its branch; instead some amount is allowed to remain, creating new pigments or colors. The brightness of these colors depends on the amount of sunlight that falls on a leaf. Thus one can truly say that the leaves enter a period where they cease their apparently self-focused sugar production activity and simply allow the sun to reflect the glory that is within them, beautifying their environment and providing inspiration to others. It is like their spirituality shining through, placed into service. And don't they look glorious?"

"Really! I suppose one needs to study these processes more closely."

"Emma, there's more. The winter season is when the tree finally rests. It withdraws its life essences from all its leaves, allowing them to fall. There is little activity within the tree except for a faint breathing, much like hibernation. But amazingly, when the tree prepares to go into its deep rest, all the leaves and flowers that are to come out next spring are already prepared, waiting within the tree as buds, ready to emerge when spring warms the earth again! Each bud is encased in a hard shell-like covering, which is but a modified form of leaf, helping to prevent the loss of moisture. Do you know what this implies?"

"You are saying that every new cycle of life is a calling forth from the experiences of a previous cycle?"

"Yes, the slumbers of the soul, that of our life-stream, and even the Godhead can be found reflected here."

"I must say I find your analogy of the colors of the fall fascinating. But what about trees in the tropics? Or the evergreens? They do not change colors."

"You are right. But there are many ways to point to the same thing. We were talking about flowering, which represents spiritual birthing. A tree flowers so that it might bear fruit. A flower falls and is replaced with a growing fruit, provided pollination was successful. Doesn't the fruit offer itself to the world? There we find the next step, that of service to the whole, as is represented by the fall colors. Next the seeds from the fruit enter into the darkness of the ground, corresponding to the rest of winter, waiting for the right conditions to germinate. And when that happens, a new tree is born as a sapling, representing spring, the beginning of another cycle. We become creators in our own right, or co-creators with God, if you will."

"Aliyah, it does make sense when you put it that way. Did you also notice another implication of this? It means that enlightenment is not the end!"

"Quite so, Emma. It is but another beginning. A branch that does not set fruit and in the end fails to create more trees has wasted its flowering. It would have been admirable, but would still fall short of its calling."

"I would have been more inclined to associate flowering with the expression of one's latent talents and abilities, not enlightenment."

"That would also be true. What you see in the tree is but a pattern, a 'universal,' if you will. The same pattern repeats or reflects itself in many avenues of life. Remember our discussion of your car and the patterns it represented? The flower does not represent spirituality only, but many other things. When it is mapped by analogy to spirituality, the meanings derived from the rest of the pattern also hold. That is why I call these patterns universals."

Emma was quick to catch on to the significance of what Aliyah was saying.

"Does this mean that one can predict our future by studying these patterns?"

"Well, yes and no, I would think. One can understand the general plans or patterns that order our lives, painting a picture at higher levels. The choice of following one plan or another is probably left to individuals."

"I'm not sure I follow you."

"Let's take humanity, for example. We have progressed from our distant origins of innocence and beauty, reflected in the garden of Eden, into a very difficult learning phase, represented in the scriptures as consuming the fruit from the tree of knowledge of good and evil. By our own analogy of the tree, after the learning phase, which is represented by the activity of the leaves, comes the flowering and then setting of fruit."

"What does it imply?"

"The flowering can be likened to a spiritual birthing of the human race, call it Christening if you like, followed by a period where our learning and experiences gathered from our difficult journey through life are placed into the service of the greater universe. Do you not see a grand plan here? Whether it is the seasons, the colors of the fall, the lifecycle of a tree, or our own progression from childhood and schooling to mature service and death, the grander implications of the pattern are the same. The fact that vegetation surrounds us everywhere is also a hint of this pattern, pointing out that this indeed is the ordained path for the race. But we seem to have our individual choices, whether to follow this plan or align ourselves with another."

"But what other plans are there to align ourselves with? I am not aware of any."

"Well, let's look at a forest and see what happens there. Besides the trees and plants you normally see, there are the parasitic plants and the poisonous ones that kill. There are also trees that are infected, diseased and which fall prematurely to the ground. Some trees are shaped into all kinds of useful things, such as this chair I am sitting on. A big tree in the forest is often a home and a shelter to a large number of creatures, just as the earth is a home to us. All these manifestations are but natural parts of an ecosystem, and one can read alternative paths of development from these. They are reflections not only of what happens in human societies, but also point to levels above, and perhaps below, as well."

"But why go through it all? Isn't it better to finish it and return to the ground?"

"Emma, the return of the tree to the ground is sure, but that is after fulfilling its greater purposes. A tree that seeks to return to the ground is sick, and it would have wasted its life. We live life because we really want to, deep within. Perhaps it is better to say that the soul or higher self wants to, or that the life-stream wants to. We are not separate from the Godhead, but an expression of it. And we as personalities speak from some of our traumas in life, making us wish we didn't have to go through these. If our purposes as individuals and as a life-stream were not worth the troubles we go through, we simply would not have taken these steps in the first place. The perspective on life is vastly different at higher levels."

Emma was silent for a while. Presently she spoke.

"Aliyah, what is it that you keep calling as the Body of God? Obviously you compare it with the Earth. But what does it mean?"

"I think it can be understood better if we look at the function of soil. The biological processes within a tree are driven by minerals and water from the soil. The mass of the tree, or most of it, is built from the air, but the processes that make it happen are driven by enzymes. These enzymes are the catalysts that build the tree, literally creating everything that makes up what we see as a tree. And these enzymes are built from minerals which are generally dissolved in water and carried up into the tree. Now take a closer look at the soil. You would see what may be called raw material, and also the remnants of old plants, trees and organisms which are being broken down and recycled."

Aliyah looked closely at Emma, wondering if she was following the discussion. Emma appeared to be listening intently.

"The analogy with the Body of God should be then obvious. This body of God is spiritual stuff, in which are present latent desires, tendencies, inclinations, emotional natures and so forth that seek expression. These ingredients may also be from prior expressions which were broken down and recycled. They are all jumbled up, mixed around and unfocused, just like the soil. Through manifestation, these tendencies are drawn-out selectively and allowed to express themselves in various forms. That very expression is creation. The primary material of expression is the mind which creates matter, corresponding to the body of the tree being precipitated primarily from the air. And this mind itself is a single mind, corresponding to the atmosphere of the planet. It is an ancient mind, if you will, quite ancient, and it takes expression in every soul and in every individual that manifests from the creative process. So this ancient mind, together with the spiritual stuff replete with latent emotions, desires and other proclivities are part of the Body of God. Creation as we know it is the expression of this Body of God. This expression is, of course, driven by the energy of the Creator, represented by the Sun itself. "

"So the Creator exists apart from us?"

"The Creator, as represented by the Sun, is the remnant of the original one source after the initial creative process. He is thus both an emergence as well as the supreme creator of all that is. The rest of creation is but His body, or His various aspects. All are one, but all are also different. The way He constantly relates to individuals can be understood by the way every leaf is nourished by sunbeams. And He appears just as silent and unnoticed in His action, as the Sun itself in planetary processes, like the seasons, the growth of a tree, or the opening of a wild flower."

"How do you know all this is true, Aliyah?"

It was Aliyah's turn to be silent. How could she convey this to Emma? From her silence she spoke:

"Personal truth is something you may not be able to relate to, Emma. But there is also objective truth. You are asking how processes at one level can reflect those at a seemingly different level. But if the Godhead exists, and life is one, how could it be otherwise? How could a tree be some freak of nature? Or the Earth simply a ball of dirt moving in the emptiness of space? Perhaps you are beginning to see a glimpse of the true nature of creation. There is much, much more we can learn about the Godhead and its ways by studying our earth. Things like, how the atmosphere came into existence and how it is sustained, the significance of gravity, the programmed death built into cells, the recycling of minerals, the weathering of rocks, the water cycle and innumerable other processes on the earth. They all have their meanings and stories to tell. That is something we can explore ourselves objectively."

In the months that followed, Aliyah found her experiences of the spirit waxing and waning unpredictably. At times she would be flung high into the pinnacles of the spirit and moments of ecstasy, but these were often followed by dry and painful periods of drought when nothing seemed to work and all her attempts to reclaim her happiness were in vain. The Lord seemed to have forsaken her, hidden Himself behind a cloud. She spent those periods in agony, trying her best to recapture that lost paradise of the spirit, when it would visit her again, but briefly. She cared little for anything else, and her purpose and passions were all directed exclusively in one direction. Failure to take hold of it and make it hers drove her into endless despair. The seasons of the spirit followed one another in succession, but the summers were too short, and the winters too long and excruciatingly painful.

And the earth went about its ordained path, forcing season after season in succession upon its inhabitants. Many species floundered and died in the winter, but many adapted in different ways. The heavens and the earth seemed to force diverse experiences on earthly inhabitants until they learned to create a proper synthesis of all the seasons within their own being. The evergreens stood majestically throughout the vagaries of the seasons, as a triangular symbol of the triune Godhead, pointing out to human beings that the ability to weather all the seasons of life equally, and the resulting temperament within, were somehow very important, indeed one of the main lessons of earthly existence. Aliyah was yet to find that balance.

In autumn, something strange happened. Aliyah would return from school and find a bouquet of flowers on her doorstep, every Friday and without fail. It was brought in the mail, and had no tags attached. They were always tropical flowers, the kind she would not normally find where she lived. She could not trace the sender despite all her efforts, and finally gave up. She loved the flowers, but who would send her tropical ones, let alone know that she fancied them?

Her thoughts turned to the stranger who had helped her escape from the mafia. He had appeared very concerned for her life, even seemed to know her well. But she knew absolutely nothing about him, or of his motives. So why did she feel that he was somehow involved?

10. Mountain

Aliyah recognizes the past and the wondrous path ahead.

S omewhere in time, on a planet circling a small yellow star
in the spiral arm of a typical galaxy with billions of stars,
an ant picked up a greenish brown leaf from an outcrop
of rock and proceeded to carry it to its nest. Making its way
through the jumble of leaves, twigs and grasses that adorned
the winding mountain path, it looked up for a moment to find
something enormous and alive regarding it with fascination. As
their eyes met, the ant paused and considered a while, its
antennae moving as it tried to make sense of this newcomer
that had intervened in its world. It soon seemed to have come
to a decision, for it proceeded along as if the intruder didn't
matter at all.

Aliyah felt a quick sense of insignificance sweep over her,
which then turned into wonder as she considered the ant's own

world of perception. How busy it was with its own! Yet it knew nothing about the size or complexity of the world around, nor experienced the emotions or thoughts of a higher being such as herself. If she could communicate with an ant, would it understand any of her concepts? The scale of being that separated her from the ant was so enormous, that any direct meaningful communication was impossible.

And yet the ant's brain was next in wonder to the human brain, for it had the capacity to learn, an amazing feat for such a tiny insect. And the way an ant colony functioned was even more amazing. The ants formed a real society under their queen, had assigned jobs, collaborated on tasks, ran nurseries for their young ones, farmed, harvested and stored, domesticated, constructed and used tools. They also cleaned and tidied up their dwellings, went to war with other colonies, some even made slaves, picked up their dead, took thought for the morrow and took care of one another. And they did all of these without someone to control and direct their actions. Here indeed was a reflection of a human society, perhaps the best possible on such a tiny scale. Still it was but a faint reflection, and no ant could possibly recognize or understand a complex and technologically advanced human society. Here was an analogy that likewise pointed to higher levels of being and organization above man, levels which Aliyah was probably utterly incapable of understanding.

Above her, beyond the mountain, was a grander cosmos, at such an enormous scale that it was literally mind-boggling. Her own comparison of scale with the ant seemed insignificant compared to that of the earth within the unfathomable vastness of the universe. Yet the universe had a homogeneous appearance throughout, with structures repeated at higher as well as lower scales, such as stars clustering into galaxies, galaxies forming clusters, and those clusters forming super clusters, and so on. Even the microcosm of the atoms with its nucleus and electrons resembled something as expansive as a solar system. There was an uncanny similarity between appearances of structures at various scales. The rocky stretch at her feet looked very much like a miniature mountain range, and the little grass and shrubs growing profusely on the ground resembled a forest. It was sometimes hard to distinguish the scale of a terrain in photographs of nature. One could be looking at a close-up image or perhaps a large-scale view. It required something else in the picture to set the scale, such as a bottle or a coin highlighting the close-up shot of some rock strata, or a person or dwelling against the backdrop of a larger terrain. And one could easily lose sense of distance in the seemingly endless rocky desert, unable to fathom whether a stretch of rock seen in the distance was just one mile away or perhaps twenty. Not only rocks, but many other features on the earth, such as trees, rivers, clouds, mountains, coastlines, snowflakes, sand dunes and other structures, tended to show a self-similarity of the whole to the smaller elements they were composed of. Did not the branch of a tree by itself look like another tree? These fractal manifestations seemed to represent a cosmic order, the working of universal principles that resulted in similar phenomena on various scales. By her system of correlations, there had to be like manifestations in the realm of the body, mind and spirit, at various scales, from the minuscule to the mind-boggling.[8] The ant moving about at her feet seemed to be a case in point.

Rising up from the hazy red of the earth under her feet were the grasses, shrubs, plants and trees that covered the earth with the colors and hues of green. Looking higher up, she encountered the milky blue vault of the sky. The colors as they progressed from the earth upward shifted from reds to greens and then to blues, frequencies of light that were progressively higher in vibration, the red color being the lowest frequency, green an intermediate one, and blue a high frequency. This progression also seemed to represent a spiritual direction, that of raising one's vibrations from involvement with earthly pleasures, signified by the low

---

[8] See chapter 'Desert'

vibrational color of red, to higher levels represented by green and blue. The green of the plants and trees were indeed growing away from the red of the earth towards the blue of the sky. The colors red, green and blue were also those the human eye was attuned to, for the cones in the retina of the eye were similarly constructed. There were three types of cones, one responding to red frequencies, one to green, and another to blue. These colors were also known as the additive primaries, for red, blue and green-colored lights could be combined to create lights of any other color. The totality of a spectrum of color, a gamut as it is known, could be created from their combinations. This was how a television tube or computer display worked, mixing red, green and blue in various proportions. This was also how the human eye functioned, to generate the sensation of other colors. Thus red, green and blue functioned as primary and essential building blocks of colors. Was it a coincidence that the same additive primaries were now stretched out before and above her? Did they not represent the very fundamental and the resulting totality of experience that the earth offered to its inhabitants? Combining red, green and blue lights in equal proportions resulted in white light, representing the bright Sun high up in the sky, such as at noon. The progression then was even more stark, from red, green and blue, to the white which represented a synthesis or union of all. *Once again the Sun represented a sublime spiritual source in her analogies!* But the visible spectrum of light was only a very narrow span within the complete range of frequencies of the solar electromagnetic spectrum, most of which extended beyond and higher than violet and could not be distinguished by her eye, representing levels of experiences as yet unfathomable to her.

And interestingly, the sunlight was not pure white to the human eye, but had a tint of yellow. Even more curiously the human eye could not distinguish the yellow frequency of light from a mixture of red and green frequencies. There were no cones in the retina for yellow, but the yellow light equally stimulated both the red and the green cones, resulting in the perception of yellow by the additive combination of red and green. Combining red, green and blue in equal proportions resulted in white light, and if the contributions of red and green were increased, the white attained a tint of yellow. The more the red and the green were given prominence, the more yellowish the light appeared. But the red and the green were also colors that immediately surrounded her in the environment, colors that represented the baser and earthly inclinations. Did the sunlight, by its yellow tint, point out a hidden significance in mundane earthly experiences?

By now, the sky was awash with color. Brilliant streaks of red, yellow and orange with hints of pink were stretched across its vast canvas, the beautifully colored strokes painted by the evening twilight, setting the stage for the Sun to drop out of the horizon. Darkness would soon engulf the land. Here was a planet of day and night, where light and darkness followed one another in succession, each calling to its own. Unlike most nearby solar-type stars that formed binary or twin-star systems, the Sun was solitary, thus casting shadows and light in equal progression on its planetary bodies. This light had always been associated with goodness, virtue and other positive aspects of the spirit. Darkness likewise evoked the ideas of selfish, destructive and negative tendencies. The earth indeed was a planet where both these aspects of the spirit co-existed, where one followed another in waxing and waning cycles, depicting an endless struggle between opposites. And to compound matters, in the midst of darkness a light existed, the light of the moon, which purportedly gave its own light but was truly not a source by itself. It represented that which confused and deluded man in the name of the light, appearing to be as big or bigger than the true source. The interplay of light, shadows and darkness on the earth was indeed a reflection of what took place therein.

But why were the skies of the dawn and the twilight so gorgeous, and most beautiful to the human eye? These moments were indeed ones of light but with a strange tint of darkness within them. The lower and supposedly baser frequencies of visible light, those of red and orange, suddenly gained prominence and an indelible beauty, as they washed the sky in the horizon, emanating from the very countenance of the solar orb which seemingly took on such colors. These were moments when darkness and light met, and the colors seemed to represent a synthesis, a union of light and darkness in a peculiar manner. The beauteous sight was a reminder to Aliyah that goodness alone in the purest sense was insufficient for the human being, for goodness also begat gullibility in most. The twilight was pointing out an essential lesson for human beings, that of integrating the best from the worlds of light and darkness, resulting in a transcendence of basic human qualities. The heavens and the earth sought to mould human beings who by choice remained pure and innocent, yet well understood the cunning and evil mind; who were pliable, but could exercise tremendous strength of will; who were gentle and peace-loving, but were great warriors who knew when and how to fight; who could weep with compassion, but could not be fooled; who could behold great injustice, and still act with restraint and foresight; who could be relentless in their pursuit of goals, not for their own benefit but for the common good; and who possessed a strong individuality, but were the essence of humility. Such seemed to be the kind of qualities that life sought to induce in the children of God who sojourned on this planet of light and darkness. The twilight, the dawn, the play of light and shade, the seasons and the yellow tint of the sunlight spoke of a great plan for mankind written in the heavens.

But how could such a synthesis be achieved? Did it not mandate that human beings of necessity experience all of the light and all of the darkness that creation has to offer? That they of necessity go through the turmoil of evil, death, despair and darkness, while holding on to their gifts of hope, faith, forgiveness and love? That would be an extremely difficult synthesis, but here it was, written in the heavens, speaking of a great plan for humankind. To meet it squarely would be no easy task for the race. It meant draining the cup of sorrows to the very last drop, allowing oneself to be tempted into the hands of the vile, the unprincipled and the diabolical; treading the byways of despair, dejection and utter desolation; finally purifying oneself by effort and the grace of God, raising above and transcending all. The temptation and the fall of man as written in the scriptures were by no means an accident, but part of a larger scheme of things, for was not the Creator also the essence of knowledge, wisdom and foresight? To be part of the plan required great courage and fortitude, as evinced by the ubiquitous plant kingdom that surrounded her. And was it not a great lesson that kingdom offered, a lesson of persistence in the face of all hardship?

The grasses were trampled, consumed, mowed down, burnt in fire, but never defeated. The shrubs and the bushes were foraged by beasts or trimmed by man, but grew back even stronger and thicker. Plants and trees spread out roots down into the earth, slowly penetrating even the hardest rock. The desert plants patiently waited their day through insufferably long periods of dryness, waiting for the promised time that they would transform the desert with their flowers. And the whole plant kingdom literally rose up against the strong pull of gravity that represented the temptations and trials of the earth. The call to fortitude, resilience, hope and courage thus resounded all about. The race would need these qualities if it were to succeed.

She slowly clambered up the mountain path, her gaze lingering on splashes of wild flowers that grew in the clearings between trees, those exquisite drops of heaven bobbing in the wind and glistening in the sunlight against the green carpet of grass. The path upwards to the summit was not a direct one, for such a path would be almost impossible for most people to climb. The practical, and indeed the most enjoyable way always meandered, going higher and higher in progression, but always within acceptable limits of endeavor. Sometimes it required a sudden and unprecedented effort, and at times the paths were slippery or appeared difficult, but one could always manage to get over them. But they were also dangerous, for one could lose one's foothold, fall far down and injure oneself. The mountain indeed held a saga of life. The higher one climbed, the cleaner was the air, and the better the panoramic view of the earth below.

And why was she so attracted to the mountains? Indeed a good majority of people shared her fascination with the mountains, which were but rock strata pushed up when the tectonic plates of the earth pressed against one another. These rock strata contained layers upon layers of sediments deposited throughout the ages of the earth, from the pre-Cambrian with its primitive life-forms, through the Mesozoic with its dinosaurs, and to the Cenozoic with its mammals and humans, with all such traces squeezed into layers of rock. Those sediments of soil had not only touched and experienced the life of those bygone ages, but they were also replete with dead and fossilized remains of organisms and creatures that lived in those times, thus capturing an extremely long evolutionary history within a few thousand feet of vertical earth. These strata also represented an evolution of being within those creatures, and as Aliyah climbed the mountain from its foothill to the summit, her feet were literally moving at an incredible speed through the past eons, spanning the very history of being on the earth, evoking deep remembrances in the unconscious. It was nostalgia of the soul. The effort also evoked a subconscious drive within to rise higher in the spirit and climb to the lofty levels of the clouds, and even past them. The path was of necessity meandering, but the way was ever forward, ever higher. The mountain served as an archetype within her being, a reminder of the past, and a call to the future.

Up in the sky and opposite the twilight sun, an evening rainbow came to life before her eyes. The light from the sun entered into billions of water drops precipitated around particles of dust, refracted within them into its composite colors, and reflected in unison those colors down towards the earth. These colors permeated the sky in regular bands. And as Aliyah moved, her eyes perceived one colorful set of bands at a time, appearing like a wondrous bow pointing man toward the heavens, with the earth as the archer. Here indeed was the most beauteous of all signs ever given to humanity, written in the skies for all to see, pointing out a very important, nay the *overarching*, purpose of the human experience: to reflect and to teach the universe, *in unison*, as a race of billions of human beings, the great and wondrous beauty of God's being when expressed through *love and love alone*. For the very symbology of refracted and reflected light through water drops directly pointed out love reflecting and expressing facets of the Godhead.[9] The rainbow was thus truly a symbol of God's love and of man's purpose. A purpose that mankind struggled with unsuccessfully for eons in its sojourn on a watery planet; one that it markedly and thoroughly failed in the misty past, bringing down on itself the deluge of the Great Flood. The human purpose mandated a long and torturous odyssey through the oceans of emotion, dragging the race through every conceivable type of feeling and sentiment, till the collective emotional experience could be subjugated, refined and purified into its most beautiful form of expression possible at the level of man, that of love. For all emotions were but varied, even twisted, expressions of this highest form of emotion that took man closest to the Godhead.

Aliyah sat down on a ledge to rest. From her vantage point on the rock could be seen a stream flowing down from the mountain peak far across, widening slowly, its waterfalls like white laces gracing the mountain side. Higher up, above the origins of the stream, were wispy tufts of white clouds that clustered and shrouded portions of the mountain. The pure waters of the stream reminded her of nobler emotions, particularly that of love. But the wispy clouds, also composed of water drops, were something of an entirely different quality. Water by itself tended to flow ever downward under the effect of gravity, slowly acquiring silt, dirt, sewage and other runoff, finally merging into the saltiness of the sea. It was the heating action of

---

[9] See chapter 'Desert'

the sun that transported waters from even the muddiest pool, the dirtiest drain and the saltiest sea into water vapor, lifting them high above into the atmosphere, transforming them into glorious clouds that offered life-giving water to the planet. Here again was a reminder about human beings, their emotions and natural proclivities which, when left to themselves, sank ever downward. But the redeeming action of grace transformed even the greatest transgressor into a benediction and an angelic source of love for many.

And the waters that finally merged into the ocean reminded her of her own spiritual experiences, when she had thought that the ultimate was experienced in a grand unification in the vastness of an ocean of consciousness. This was but an identification with the collective consciousness of all, a common denominator which was also evolving and progressing at its own level. The waters of the oceans were too salty, salt being a very earthy element, and not meant for human consumption. In fact prolonged exposure was dangerous to the physiology of the body. Likewise, her own ingrained natures, proclivities and unwanted habits had persisted despite her deepest spiritual experiences, and in fact she had even acquired an ego of accomplishment, a saltiness that colored her personality. This could now be her undoing. It took the redeeming action of grace in the form of difficult circumstances, signified by the heat of the sun, to slowly purify her of those tendencies and take her up higher. Mystics throughout the ages had often reported such a turn of events, and such exceedingly trying times were known to many as the dark night of the soul. She herself had been going through similar experiences and it pointed to a major imbalance within her personality, one which life set about to correct in an effort to restore balance.

It took time, but she finally understood that earthly life had to be given as much importance as those heavenly incursions, because the very synthesis of earth and heaven within was crucial to her sojourn here. Like the majestic mountain from which she now gazed into infinity, she was meant to have her head above the clouds, her heart amidst them, and her feet firmly on the earth.

There came also the recognition that there were many more realms and modes of being, indescribable and beyond her wildest dreams, and stretching higher into the heavens, where humanity was called to explore and learn, to live, to love and to create. The journey back home to the Godhead was indeed a circle, and it did not mean going back to one's beginnings by undoing everything that was built up through the ages. Instead, it meant going forward and completing the circle. Humanity was being prepared.

Aliyah began her descent along the mountain path. The sun was setting and shadows crept along the trail. Looking down to the side, she could see the sprawl of the city suburbs far away. On an impulse she decided to leave the trail and take a downward path through the trees. She clambered down the steep slope, moving from tree to tree, leaning against each in turn before moving down to the next one.

Then she heard it, the muffled sound of drums echoing through the forest. She stopped to listen. The drumming started as a slow and simple beat that gradually increased in complexity and tempo. Soon it reverted to forms she knew, like rumba and the rhythms of the cha-cha. The sounds seemed to come from a direction to the west. She decided to investigate and started heading down that way.

She moved forward and down and the sounds became louder. The terrain here was rockier than the rest and made progress difficult. But she was very curious. Who on earth would be drumming in the middle of the forest at this time? For what reason?

All of a sudden the drumming stopped. She strained and listened. What could have happened? She could hear nothing, except for bird calls and the wind rushing through the trees. She took another step, lost her balance and grabbed on to a tree branch to prevent herself from falling. For a moment she managed to hold on, but the branch broke and she fell headlong down the rocky slope, triggering a small avalanche. She hit the ground, rolled and came forcefully to a stop against an old tree trunk.

She tried to get up and pain shot through her ankles. Looking down, she could see that both her ankles were bleeding, possibly from impact with rock. She tried to get up again and found she couldn't. Her ankles were badly hurt. She would have to crawl and it was now almost dark. No one would find her there and soon it would get too cold. There had been stories of people being lost and freezing to death overnight in these mountains. Recognition dawned on her that she too might face the same peril. Agitated, she shouted for help, only to realize that there was no one around within earshot. Her frustration now turned to tears. She sobbed, lay down on her side and started to pray.

There was movement in the shadows. Someone or something was watching her. Instinctively, she sat up. Across her and atop a rock was a dark, silent figure, looking down at her.

"Help me!" she cried out. "I can't walk."

The figure descended the rock with cat-like ease and came closer to where she was lying on the ground. Then came the voice,

"Didn't I tell you to get the hell out of here?"

Aliyah gazed in stunned silence as the figure moved into the light. She was looking at none but her beloved, miraculously back from the dead. She stared, disbelieving, bewilderment and shock flooding through her system. Voiceless, her lips tried to frame a question.

He said nothing, but walked over, took her forcibly into his arms and kissed her. In a fire of ecstatic emotion, she melted into his embrace.

11. Tree of Knowledge

Aliyah finds hints of deep connections between Darwinian and spiritual evolution.

The terrain was gray and foreboding with undulating hills that rose up to reflect the light, with their valleys shrouded in darkness. There were no grass, shrubs, winds, insects or anything of that sort, except some trees that sparsely dotted the landscape. The sky was an azure blue, with no clouds in sight. Observed from high above, the land looked arid and dry, inhospitable to life. But on closer inspection, one could distinguish some movement on the ground, as though something were alive. There were indeed many little creatures scurrying hither and thither on this terrain. They were crablike in appearance, moved about on many legs and had antennae that sensed their surroundings. Some of these little creatures were moving about excitedly and in a hurry. They seemed to have sensed that time was running short, and that something ominous was about to come, that their world was about to end in a catastrophic destruction.

On the horizon ahead was a great light, a hope of salvation for many of the creatures that existed in this strange landscape. The light was far away, farther than they could hope to reach by their own efforts. Yet it seemed a worthy goal, something to strive for, something that might offer protection from the disaster soon to strike their world.

Life in this world was not easy, for there were strange things afoot. The creatures had to be very careful where they went, for huge snakes would often rise up from the ground in a flash and swallow many. There were many kinds of snakes, some yellow, some blue, some with rings and some with spots. They nestled, hidden under the ground at unsuspected locations, waiting for an unfortunate creature that would stumble into their lair. Those that were not sensitive to the subtle scent given off by a snake were caught and swallowed quickly. Curiously, the snakes did not kill, but instead dragged the victim through their insides to the tail end and defecated it far away from the light on the horizon. Their intent was to make sure that the creatures never came to the light.

The creatures were not without help. There were also in the land many friendly birds that lived on the trees that dotted the landscape. These birds offered help by carrying many of the creatures some distance towards the light, to the edge of their own individual territories. Some of the birds were red of plumage, some blue, some yellow and some black. And they strove to pick up these creatures, fly past the lairs of the snakes, and carry their burden onward, closer to the light on the horizon. But like most birds, they were limited to their own territories and could only take the creatures so far. From there the creatures had to make it on foot, dreading the snakes and hoping to find another friendly bird in the new territory. So there was hope.

But there was trickery afoot. The forces of light and those of darkness had made a strange pact. The dark ones had demanded a representative species among the birds as their own, and they offered a snake species in return. The bargain was accepted, and the result was deadly. The red birds, which also appeared to be saviors of their world, were instead agents of destruction, as they delivered their burden not to safe ground but very close to the lairs of a red snake. And the blue snakes, though appearing fiery like dragons, swallowed up and deposited their prey away from the light, but close to a tree where fast-moving blue birds nested.

Such was the strange agreement that existed, unknown to these creatures, between the forces of darkness and those of the light. For it was a crucial test of discernment. Would the creatures learn to recognize the snakes as foes and the birds as friends? For the creatures were very primitive, not knowing what a snake or a bird was and what they represented. When these creatures first began their existence in this world, they had not tasted the fruit of the tree of knowledge, of knowing good and evil. Would they learn to distinguish those now? By projecting complex manifestations of good and evil, the world seemed to test them continuously. Could they discern the truth about the red birds and the blue snakes, or would they fall victim to the forces of darkness?

Indeed, many could make the distinction, Aliyah noted, as she watched the creatures move quickly toward the light on the horizon, avoiding snakes and helped onward by birds. Some even looked for blue snakes to hitch a ride through their bellies, for they knew that they offered an easy way to get to the fast-moving blue birds. And they knew the red birds by their calls. But there were also many that failed to make the grade. While they did recognize birds as friends, they failed to see the treachery of those red in plumage and were doomed to destruction.

"This is how instinct evolves," smiled Robert, as he clicked on a mouse button and froze the display. She was looking at a computer screen, where a simulation had been in progress. The landscape, creatures, snakes and birds, all existed as concepts within a computer. Robert had created an artificial world, populated it with creatures, and created his own laws that governed the habitats of the snakes and birds. He had also set up the strange interrelationship between some of the snakes and birds.

"The behavior of each creature is driven by a genetic code embedded in them," Robert explained. "When I started, all the creatures in my world were endowed with random genetic information, which means they were practically useless and could not function in their world. They were like Adam and Eve thrust out of Eden, freshly minted, having no clue as to what to do in a harsh world. But after evolution through many generations, they came to learn about their environment, its temptations and pitfalls, as well as its good things. And they used that knowledge to their advantage."

"So how come I didn't see any evolution happen?" asked Aliyah.

It was Theo who answered. "What you just saw were creatures born after about ten thousand generations of evolution, and according to the principles of mutation and natural selection."

Theo had brought Aliyah to this alife lab with a specific intent: to convince her how powerful and accurate the scientific principles of evolution were. Even though he found many of her spiritual notions interesting, the arguments were not strong enough to dissuade him from his established views, especially given his academic background. This disparity between them led to a fair amount of disagreement on matters of evolution and consciousness, which sometimes flared up in hot discussions. Theo now hoped to settle the matter once and for all. He wanted her to be fully compatible with him; after all, the couple were soon to be married.

And to this end, he had made some progress, for she was greatly impressed by what she saw. Before her was a stark demonstration of the creative power of evolution through mutation and selection, even if it were a simulation running on a computer.

Robert picked up her question and added, "You see, the original ancestors were practically useless and most could not even move, let alone distinguish a snake from a bird. But there were a few among them that fared slightly better than the others and managed at least to move about, even if it were a single step. Now this artificial world is visited by periodic catastrophes that wipe out everything, and their only safe haven is at the horizon where the light is."

"What has the light got to do with it?" she asked.

"The light is just a prop for the visuals," laughed Robert. "I like it, and it kind of makes the whole thing melodramatic. Reaching the horizon is their ultimate goal, whether there is light or not. Now after a world has ended, I pick up the survivors and the best among them are joined together in marriage."

Aliyah was confused, "Marriage? You mean these creatures are male and female?"

"Not really!" laughed Robert. "That's just a figure of speech. It is just that I take them in pairs and create a new generation from each pair. For this, I apply a random crossover of their genetic information so that the new creatures would have characteristics of both their so-called parents. During this process I also introduce some random mutations into their genes, much like biological reproduction."

"I see. So you destroy a world and then repopulate it with a new generation! Reminds me of Noah's flood. But why do you need to destroy those worlds?"

"Without death, there is no evolution. Perhaps you can liken it to Noah's flood, or whatever you'd like to call it. I consider all those creatures as representing a single species and I need to visit them with death so that the better ones get to survive and reproduce and finally get smart enough to distinguish the snakes and birds properly." Robert paused, then laughed and continued, "Those who choose to eat from the tree of knowledge of good and evil must be visited by death. Of course, there is no death in one sense, for the genes continue on."

"What do you mean, without death there is no evolution?"

"Well, without some way to select the better adapted ones for reproduction, a species cannot improve. In nature, selection comes about through death, where the lesser fit are taken out of the game. The term we use for this is 'selective pressure', where the environment forces the species to evolve certain characteristics, under the threat of death."

"Amazing!" she breathed. "So you are saying that you evolved intelligence from nothing? That these creatures, simply through evolution, discovered the true nature of the birds and the snakes, and even the alliance between them?"

"I call it instinct rather than intelligence," replied Robert. "Intelligence, as you call it, is lost with death. Instinct has roots within the genes and thus survives across generations. These critters are wired to behave as their genes dictate. Evolution over many generations created successful behavioral patterns that let them survive better in my world."

"So they recognize red birds instinctively?"

"Yes. Many of these critters are wired such that when they sense a red bird, it is considered dangerous, and a blue snake, benevolent. So what you see is the development of innate knowledge of the environment and about creatures and patterns that exist there. That is instinct."

"But how do they know that they should go towards the light?" asked Aliyah.

"That's a good question. First of all, they do not know, but they have this built-in drive given by their evolution. In natural selection it is the environment that dictates whether a creature is fit or not. Here, I make the decision, which is essentially saying that I want them to learn to distinguish between what might be called the right choices and wrong choices, even in cases where the patterns are not obvious. It is my definition of their fitness, for I am God in this world."

"Wow! That's fantastic!" Aliyah exclaimed as she mulled over this piece of information. "You mentioned genes. What are theirs made of?"

"Oh, their 'genes' are computer instructions to do various tasks, like move around, sense what is ahead, compare sensory input with something in memory and so on. Somewhat like a robot. When I started the simulation, they all had random instructions in their genes, meaning they did nonsensical things, like moving backward, going round and round, oscillating, or not moving at all. There was little coherent behavior. They had no idea about birds or snakes. But all I had to do was pick the survivors for reproduction and start again."

"Hmm... but why don't you let the snakes kill those that failed, instead of keeping them till the end of their world?"

"Well, I chose to do so because there might yet be redeeming instructions within an apparently failing creature's genes that might cause it to tumble back into the light. You see, each creature is quite unique, and the instructions it carries may have all sorts of complexities. So I deemed it fit that I let the so-called weeds grow along with my crops. After my harvest, those that are still found to be weeds are," Robert paused and grinned, "cast into the fire!"

"But you said that the original ancestors could only move about a few steps towards the light. So how did they survive the destruction of their world?"

"Ah! That was an act of providence! My computer program looked into the initial populations and found the ones that had made some rudimentary progress, like a few steps towards the light. They were transported to safety before their world was destroyed. I had to lower the bar there; otherwise there was no hope of getting them ultimately to where I wanted. But as soon as the first creature made it to the light, there was no longer any such need, for I was sure that many of their descendants would follow suit."

"I see. So how would those of the later generations compare with the older ones who managed to reach the light?"

"In *general* you can say that the later generations do better, because they have better adapted. But it is also quite possible to backslide across generations, specifically due to the genetic cross-over and mutations resulting in an un-learning. Also my choice to keep the degenerate ones until the end of their world can also affect the gene pool adversely, because many of them that barely made it through would pass on unwanted genes as well. Now if you were to place individuals from a much older generation along with the ones you've just seen and run my world again, you can truly say that many that were first shall be last, and many that were last shall be first," laughed Robert.

Aliyah thought about that. Then she had another question, "Did these creatures change their appearance, create new species, for example?"

"Oh, not in this simulation. The selection pressure that I exerted was towards reaching the horizon where the light is, and how well they recognized and tackled the hurdles on the way. The focus here is on their behavior, not physical appearance."

Theo intervened to add to the discussion, "But other researchers have done computer simulations where they focused on bodily structures. And they evolved creatures with long legs for walking, fins and paddle-like structures for swimming and so on; all with Darwinian selection of course."

"Yes!" added Robert, "and then there are other simulations where parasites appear automatically through mutation. Then follows a kind of evolutionary arms-race where the creatures and the parasites try to outwit each other, co-evolving all kinds of strategies. Yup, there are many interesting results from research in this field. Similar techniques are also used to discover solutions to engineering problems."

Aliyah found the last statement highly interesting.

"Solutions to engineering problems? Do you mean to say that evolution is a mechanism that finds solutions to problems?"

"Well, that is a dangerous statement," replied Robert, "It is true that evolution through variation and selection is a valid scientific method of finding solutions to a given problem. But that is possible *only* if there is a way of evaluating a solution for its merit, like ten percent correct, fifty percent correct, ninety percent correct and so on. This can be used to create a selective pressure to move towards a hundred-percent-correct solution. In my worlds, I could rank my creatures based on their ability to move towards the light and how well they recognized and avoided pitfalls."

"I see. Now why do you need mutations? Why can't just the pressure of selection alone do it?"

"Oh no! Mutations and cross-over are very important, for they are the only source of variation, or variety in behavior in my world. It is these that create different tendencies or natures within my creatures. You know, to explore the unexplored, express new facets of behavior hitherto untouched. Without them, evolution can get stuck in a local maxima and never progress further."

"Local maxima? What does that mean?"

"Well, it is easier to describe with a picture. Consider evolution as climbing a hill. The higher you get, the better your solution. But when you reach the summit, you see that there is another hill close by, its summit far above yours. It represents a better solution to the problem. You have done very well, getting to where you are now. But you have no way of getting to the other hill without climbing down first. And you can't, because your genes will need to regress and back-slide, dragging you down the hill and then up the other. You are now stuck in what we call a local maxima, unable to get to the bigger one."

"So how do you get to the bigger one?"

"The answer is mutation. Mutation essentially creates variety so that many hills can be explored simultaneously, and it can also force you down from the top of your small hill so you can try another. And this is what parasites in other simulations also help accomplish."

"I think I understand mutations now. But how do parasites help? Aren't they destructive or evil, preventing progress?"

"From a higher perspective, *not at all!* To the creatures themselves they might be anathema, but in the higher scheme of things they are actually *beneficial* to the gene pool. They make sure that the race to the summit happens much faster, and even drags creatures down from a local maxima into the valleys so that there is again potential for progress by climbing up another hill. And they make quick work of the congenitally weak ones."

"So if you take an individual perspective, parasites are deadly and evil, but from a collective evolutionary perspective they are actually beneficial? And they even arise spontaneously?"

"Correct! And it would be surprising if they did not arise spontaneously. They are part and parcel of evolution."

"I see. So mutations generate variety, a selection process of reward and punishment ensures that progress is made, and parasites greatly speed up the process. Is that correct?"

"Well, yes, if you consider evolution in the context of solving a given problem. The term reward and punishment may be considered as applicable to genes as they wax and wane in the gene pool. But for the creatures that they represent, it is a matter of life or death! And it is important to note that evolution in nature, for all we know, is open-ended, meaning that there are no pre-defined sets of problems out there for which existence wants us to find, or become, solutions. The environment is the deciding factor in all cases."

"I see, so evolution is, what shall I say, without any motive or purpose?"

"Yes. We know of none and there can't be any. Now if I were to attribute purposeful evolution to nature, which I would not obviously..." Robert went on, "I would say that nature is not too concerned about individuals per se, but rather with a species as a *whole*."

"Hmm... That is very interesting," Aliyah nodded gently. "And what did you finally conclude from your simulations?"

"Ah! That is a very good question," beamed Robert. "Are you ready for this?"

"Sure," she smiled.

"Okay, now note that all of my worlds were governed by unwritten rules or laws. No two worlds were identical but the laws behind them were always the same. Understand what I mean?"

"Well, I can guess!"

"To take an example, the natural world we see around us here differs from what you see in, say Tibet or India, but the laws of nature are still the same. Similarly the worlds seen by different generations of my species were all different, but the nature of the snakes, the birds and their *relationships* were always the same. It was never the same snake or the same bird in all the subsequent worlds, and they were never even in the same locations. The size of their population varied as well. The birds never flew the same distances or nested in the same trees. Nor were the trees always in one place, for their population, too, varied. The same was true of the snakes as well. The rules or laws of their relationships were *hidden*, as it were."

"I see."

"Now the amazing part! My creatures were able to discover those laws and use them to their advantage, *without* being told, and without any engineering on my part. All I provided was the potential and the drive. Isn't that wonderful? Now look at Mother Nature, run by laws such as those we know of in physics. What is a possible conclusion?"

"Perhaps evolution has discovered many laws of nature and applied them in its creatures?"

"Precisely! I am convinced that nature is *extremely* high-tech, way beyond our current understanding. Consider photosynthesis, the key to life on earth, and we are still struggling to unravel its nitty-gritty details. Or take an even simpler example. Apples float, whereas potatoes sink. Nature discovered the laws of buoyancy before we did, and found a way to transport seeds of life across the waters. You can bet that it has even used quantum effects somewhere along the way, perhaps in our very minds and brains!"

While this was an interesting conclusion, Aliyah felt that much was left unsaid. The discovery and application of natural laws through evolution came as quite a surprise. Here was a tree of knowledge indeed! Was it possible that physical evolution was an analogue, a reflection, of a greater evolution above? Was there a greater tree of knowledge in the spirit that was being explored? Were there selective pressures forcing spiritual evolution towards the light? For her last question, there was indeed a force she was aware of, a spiritual law that was often called *the law of sowing and reaping*.

"I hope Robert helped clarify things for you!" commented Theo, as they walked towards the parking lot.

"It's fantastic!" replied Aliyah dreamily. "I never suspected evolution to be such a powerful force."

Theo smiled happily and pressed her closer to him. He felt he had finally made his point.

For Aliyah, the discussion had raised more questions than it had answered, and opened up new vistas for inquiry. She was now determined to explore further.

12. Path

Aliyah comes to understand physical and spiritual evolution as analogues of each other.

mma found the notion ridiculous. How could physical evolution possibly be the analogue of a spiritual evolution? To her, nature was always red in tooth and claw. If God existed, He had to be the very essence of goodness. There cannot be such a thing as the survival of the fittest or one species devouring another in a universe ruled by such a God. She voiced her objection:

"Don't you know that the very notion of evolution is a strong argument against God and creationism? So how can you use it as an analogy? It is quite the antithesis of what you are proposing."

Aliyah considered this a while. She understood well the objections Emma was raising; for these had been part of her own thoughts till recently. But now she was beginning to see another pattern emerge from her system of correspondences.

"Let me try to put it this way. Evolution of a species is really the evolution of the gene pool, isn't it? Physical bodies are but organized matter, the expression of genes. Bodies appear to grow and die, but the gene pool continues on, expressing itself in newer forms."

"How does that have any bearing on the spiritual side?"

"Well, think of an analogous gene pool existing at a higher level, consisting of what we may call spiritual genes. These spiritual genes, being fundamental units of consciousness rather than physical matter, then represent natures, attributes, desires and aspirations latent or hidden within a given spiritual essence. So we can think of a spiritual essence or being as an organized and manifested consciousness, an expression of its spiritual genes."

Emma felt this time Aliyah had gone too far. Her analogies in the past had sounded plausible, but this time Emma simply could not move ahead.

"Really! From where did you cook up these spiritual genes? Do they exist in any spiritual lore? I've never heard anything of that sort."

"I guess one could use certain Eastern terms[10] rather than 'spiritual gene' and 'expression'. But those terms are so loaded with various religious connotations, that it wouldn't be easy to view them outside their context. Let's keep it simple and assume that this is not something totally strange to the human ear!"

"Are you saying that there are more fundamental elements behind our consciousness?"

"So to speak. By analogy, our consciousness may be considered as an expression of these fundamental elements or spiritual genes,

---

[10] See 'Samskara' and 'Vasana' in the glossary

if you will. And these genes continue on, taking new expressions of consciousness."

"Continue on in new expressions? That sounds like those concepts of reincarnation where a soul manifests repeatedly in different lives."

"Not quite reincarnation, Emma. Let's study the physical process a bit more closely." Aliyah paused to gather her thoughts.

"While the genes do express again," she continued, "it is never the same body or the same combination of genes that manifest. Many genes are borrowed from the pool to manifest, so to speak, and many are repressed. Likewise it is never the exact same composition of spiritual genes that manifest in a subsequent consciousness, and therefore it is never the same entity that is projected forth again."

"You mean they are similar but not the same."

"Yes. The newly projected spiritual consciousness might have many of the same tendencies as an earlier one due to the spiritual genes it carries. In fact, the process is somewhat like a leaf withering on a branch and a new bud forming elsewhere on the same branch. The essences within these two leaves are never quite the same. Therefore you cannot really call it reincarnation as it is conventionally known, though there are similarities with that notion."

"Aliyah, that's quite an analogy! Bodies die, but what is it that dies in your analogy?"

"Well, the physical death we speak of is quite a humanistic concept! It has managed to color our perceptions about life greatly. If you look at our bodies in a clinical or scientific manner, then you can see that each new body originates from another one and is a part and parcel of the parent, except that they are physically separated. In fact, the body never really dies. All of our bodies are the manifestations of one ancestral body, which has self-replicated, grown, mutated, and transformed into billions of bodies over eons of time. If you remember the biblical story, even Eve was made from Adam's body."

"But a child grows and new cells are formed, apart from the parent. It is a new body then, isn't it?"

"The same thing happens in your own body too. Your body also grows, and the cells are replaced every seven years or so. That is a process of rejuvenation or continuation. You don't consider yourself new every seven years, do you?"

Emma smiled at that.

"So you can see that the body does continue, but each line of continuation is a variation on the theme. That is, the genes that are expressed with each new expression are not quite the same as those of its predecessor. Some of them could even be ancient and may have remained unexpressed in the gene pool for a very long time."

"So you are saying that physical bodies are immortal?"

"More or less. There is definitely apparent death, an apparent discontinuity of physical existence. But if you look at the process, you see that the body does continue on in newer expressions. The apparent death is like a leaf withering and falling away from a branch. Of course, a lineage can be wiped out or be extinct, but there are always other manifestations of the ancestral body that continue."

Emma was not about to let go of this.

"Aliyah, this sounds quite suspect. It does not correlate well with what I have learnt about the theory of evolution. One of the key principles there is that acquired natures are not inherited; they are not transmitted to offspring. If an animal learns to do something useful, its genes however are unaffected and therefore it is unable to transfer the same genetically to its children. That goes against the very concept of spiritual learning. We are supposed to be learning through spiritual evolution, aren't we?"

"Emma, hard as it sounds, that analogy also has its truth. Acquiring learning or knowledge is only of utilitarian use, and it does not continue on in subsequent generations of a spiritual essence. You don't see babies coming in worldly-wise do you? Only those experiences that change the expressions of the soul are worth inheriting. These experiences represent internal changes in the personality or soul, whether good or bad. They are like mutations within the spiritual genes, changes that were truly made deep within oneself. Those are the only changes we carry away with us."

"That sounds like one cannot change by oneself at all. For that would mean a self-created mutation. But biological organisms are not capable of producing mutations within themselves. So your analogy fails there, doesn't it?"

"Not quite. There are indeed self-directed mutations. Simple bacteria can create and even speed-up mutation rates within themselves under stressful conditions. Stressful conditions! That's an example for you. Look up research annals and you will see. But let's not go too much by popular interpretations of science. They also change."

Emma paused and reflected on this. It was getting all too confusing. How could a spiritual evolution exist, paralleling the physical? It was supposed to be perfect in the spirit, where one would consider the physical world as an anomaly, a problem from which one could escape. She voiced her confusion:

"So where does all this lead? Why should there be such spiritual evolution at all?"

Aliyah was quiet for a while. This was one of those existential questions anyone could pose.

"To answer that, let us study the correspondence again. Where does physical evolution lead? It is an exploration, seeking perfection within an environment; the perfection of the gene pool, if you will, though often this drive is described in terms of survival. It is by manifestation of a body that the properties of a gene are discovered. Until then, they are unknown, unexpressed. But once a gene is expressed, its fruit is known, and then it is fostered, repressed or removed from the pool as fit."

"So?"

"So is spiritual evolution – an exploration through manifestation, a discovery of one's own nature and also of the universe, a purging of that which is unsuitable, and the seeking of perfection. You can think of physical evolution as one ancestral body expressing

141

itself in uncountable billions of bodies, whether they be amoebas, insects, animals or humans - seeking the limits of physical existence, continuously evolving. Likewise you can also think of spiritual evolution as one ancestral being or God expressing itself in uncountable billions of souls, discovering itself and seeking the limits of experience, continuously evolving."

"So is that what God is, then? The sum total of all the beings that exist?"

"No, Emma! The Godhead is much more than that. To see that is not difficult if you study the analogy of physical bodies in proper context."

Aliyah continued, "In the final analysis, all physical bodies are one with mother earth, for in her they live and move and have their essence. And the earth which represents the manifested Godhead is intimately connected with the Sun that in turn represents the creator-sustainer aspect of the Godhead. Isn't it the sun's energy that drives all physical evolution? It is the totality of the solar system that represents the Godhead, not just the earth alone or the bodies alone. So you can see that God is much more than the ancestral being that we talked about. That ancestral being is, however, an integral aspect of the Godhead as it manifests."

"But why all the pain and traumas associated with evolution? Nature is really cruel, isn't it? Look at all the creatures that are killed and eaten! Surely no God would allow that! How could a spiritual evolution be anything similar?"

"Well, appearances can be deceiving. Let us look at the processes again, considering only the physical. A tree draws minerals from the earth into itself, which is part of the tree for a while and then exits the tree at some point in time. The tree essentially provides a more complex organization and function to the minerals. Likewise, an animal eats a plant, and the matter in the plant is now given a greater organization within the animal body. Follow so far?"

"Yes. You are saying that the food-chain represents a progress-ively greater organization of matter, a transformation."

"Precisely. You can consider eating as upgrading the eaten stuff into a higher level of organization, until the matter exits the body through metabolism or death. A similar analogy is true in the realm of spiritual consciousness as well."

"What do you mean?"

"Let's say a bird swallows a fish. The process helps temporarily upgrade the spiritual consciousness of the fish, as the two blend together as one for a while before being separated again. The fish is given a greater perspective on life for a while, namely that of the bird, which is a more advanced species, just considering evolutionary history alone."

Emma stared as though she couldn't believe her ears.

"It is thus an impetus for the fish to progress further. In fact, it is an excellent arrangement that prompts a spiritual essence to evolve further, seek higher ground. The fish offers the gift of physical nourishment, though temporary, and the bird offers the gift of a higher consciousness, also temporary. That experience is not unlike that which spiritual practitioners describe as higher states of consciousness, but those are on a different scale."

Emma, unable to contain her incredulity any longer, burst out, "This has got to be the worst I've heard so far, even for an analogy! Forget your spiritual gene, but this one really takes the cake! The whole thing is way-out wacky!"

"Not quite, Emma! In the case of lower order life forms, there is little by way of strong emotions to prevent such a merging from happening. Of course this happens only when the life form is consumed alive, such as a frog swallowing a fly, or a lizard dining on a cricket. What happens at the physical level also happens at a higher level. In fact, it extends to even lower orders, such as plants and fruits. Why do you think some trees grow more fruit in places where people can see them?"

Emma frowned for a moment, but soon recovered.

"So am I downgraded if a python gulps me down for dinner? And what about all the carnivores that have evolved, terrorizing other species?"

"You are right. There is no upgrading or downgrading of consciousness there. The emotional stress in the prey makes any such merging impossible."

"Good! You are beginning to make a little sense. Just a little, mind you. Now how do you explain carnivores?"

"Well, do you remember our analogy of photosynthesis? [11] A tree is precipitated directly from the air. Only a small contribution to its body matter comes from solid earth. But in all appearance it seems to have been formed out of the body of the earth! You can see that the photosynthesis process by analogy reveals the creative influence of mind, emotion and spirit on matter. Now apply the same concept on the spiritual genes and try to see how they might affect the physical species."

"You mean physical evolution is driven by spiritual evolution?"

"That would be a good conclusion. What it means then is that the Godhead does not manifest a carnivorous tiger, a cannibalistic spider or a blood-sucking mosquito so as to have some morbid fun! Those species have arisen due to similar natures that are harbored within their spiritual essences. Those tendencies and natures are then reflected in the physical. It is a mechanism that allows those spiritual essences to discover their spiritual genes, the natures they harbor."

This went beyond anything Emma had expected. It implied that carnivores were but natural manifestations of evolving spiritual essences, essences which drove the evolution of their physical counterparts. But still there were more vexing problems.

"Aliyah, I think you have pushed back the problem from the physical to a higher level. That still doesn't explain why nature often appears cruel. Can you watch a leopard killing a deer and say the same thing you are saying now?"

Aliyah was silent again. There seemed to be no end to Emma's questions.

---

[11] See chapter 'Sky'

"Emma, let me give you an analogy instead. Last month I visited my hometown. And you know what? My old school is still there! All the kids of my age went through it and moved on. But the school still remains, looking more or less as I remember it, only the buildings now look older. But there are new kids, new teachers, new equipment; almost everything inside is new. But outwardly the school looks like very little has changed since I left it."

"I am not getting your drift. What has the school to do with carnivores?"

"Well the school is what we may call a system. A system is an organization or a scheme of things through which various elements move in and out, following certain laws. Think of a tornado, for instance. We see it as a single body of air, moving along, spewing destruction. But if you look at the air molecules in that body, we see that a molecule enters the system of the tornado, goes through it and then exits. More air molecules enter. The tornado is sustained by the air molecules that flow in and out and gives the appearance of being a single body as it moves. Follow me?"

"Yes."

"Likewise the school gives the appearance of remaining the same throughout the years. But it is never the same air molecules that make up a moving tornado, and never the same kids or teachers that make up the system of a school. Air molecules enter and exit the tornado, and new air molecules continue to enter and exit, even as kids and teachers also enter and exit schools. The school appears to remain the same, and the tornado too appears to remain the same."

"You are saying that applies to carnivores? That carnivores are a system like a school or a tornado?"

"What you see as a leopard killing a deer in nature is indeed such a system. It is never the same leopard or the same deer that you see again, and the suffering you see has no continuity. Each system has its insights to offer to spiritual essences. And they move in and out of these systems. But we tend to see only the peripheral appearance, the outward system as such, which seems to persist over long periods of time."

"There are many such systems?"

"There are innumerable such systems that spiritual entities can choose from, to live in and experience. It is not unlike the various systems that we see on the earth, like the tropics, the grasslands, the deserts, the mountains, the lakes and so forth, which come into existence automatically through interaction of the elements. And in such wide variety of terrain, you get to choose your vacation spots, don't you? Likewise, a great assortment of life-systems exist, and they are used by only those entities that want to or benefit from them. And most importantly, it is through the very existence of such *diversity* that evolution is possible."

"But what benefit at all could occur from a carnivore system?"

"Well, every system needs to be compatible with the spiritual genes that express through them. By such manifestation, one can observe one's own natures much better, as it provides great insight. But let us look at just the suffering aspect of the leopard-deer system. There is again a possible analogy with a school."

"Like?"

"Compare with our description of the school for a moment, and the teachers there. Now the teachers were also students once. One cannot teach what one hasn't learnt oneself at least to some degree. Simply put, going through an experience or emotion is a prerequisite for being able to relate to it successfully."

"I guess that is true," acknowledged Emma.

"Now compassion is something one cannot generally learn until one has gone through situations of suffering. Even the term compassion means to suffer with. You cannot really empathize with a beggar in the streets of India unless you yourself could understand that predicament."

"You mean the carnivore system helps to instill compassion?"

"Among many other things, yes. Spiritual essences lacking in aspects of love and compassion can particularly benefit from inhabiting such systems. In general there are very many purposes being served by any single system."

Emma found these concepts boggling her mind. Was it that nature was quite the opposite of what she had imagined? Was it indeed benign? Was there indeed an evolution in the spirit, paralleling the physical?

Then she had an even deeper question.

"If that is true, Aliyah, why should nature appear to us often as bloodthirsty and merciless? Why should it hide its benign nature?"

"Well it does manage to reflect our own natures, no?" Aliyah smiled, and then continued:

"That view is simply a result of the framework of thought we have adopted. However that framework of thought is not wrong to have. Consider that spiritual evolution by definition *requires* this freedom of thought and expression, the ability to explore various modes of existence, viewpoints and so on. This is how *variety* comes into existence. And variety or variation is a fundamental *necessity* for evolution, whether physical or spiritual."

"So spiritual evolution is, what shall I say, unbiased?"

"Yes. The spiritual universe does not suppress one viewpoint or one mode of being in favor of another, but offers a level playing field where multiple viewpoints and modes of being can be fostered simultaneously. However suppression or selection and expansion do come about through the evolutionary process."

"Are you saying that our sciences, religions, and ethics are acceptable to spiritual life, along with evil, suffering and other perversions? That atheist, agnostic and religious modes of life are equally acceptable?"

"It is not a question of acceptability. These modes of life are indeed required to make progress, to understand ourselves and to evolve at all. And what we see today will change towards the better, and that which is unfit will be discarded after having understood it completely, inside out. That is the perfect way that unfolds and ends in perfection, for spiritual evolution is directed towards the Godhead."

"You are saying that life is perfect?" Emma asked incredulously.

"From a very high perspective, yes, life is indeed perfect. But such a view does not yet apply to our perspectives as human beings. We do have our noses to the grindstone." She laughed.

Emma pondered this for a while. Where was it all leading then?

"So there is a purpose to life, is there?"

"There is not one, Emma, but an almost infinitude of purposes, and at various levels. If anything had only a single purpose, then it would cease to exist as soon as that purpose is fulfilled. There are purposes we serve simultaneously at the levels of individuals, families, societies, cultures, nations and even at the level of mankind. By analogy there are even greater purposes at still higher levels and far beyond, which cannot even be expressed in human terms, for they would convey no meaning to us right now. We would not be able to relate to them at present, any more than an ant could relate to our conversation."

"But isn't there a final, ultimate purpose?"

"At the highest level there is always the Godhead, and our great return to it. But that return would be less glorious if we did not carry with us the fruit of our experiences. Emma, don't miss the point. Life *is* the reason and purpose for life."

13. Ovum

Aliyah finds the origin of all creation reflected in an embryo.

Microwave Universe Map Source: NASA/WMAP Science Team

In the beginning there was the unknown, the unexpressed. Formless, yet having a form, lifeless, yet holding the very keys to life, unaware of itself, yet containing all the potential for awareness, not knowing anything, yet with the potential to know all - it existed and it was. Then a deep stirring arose in the unknown, like a Word that represented meaning, intent, desire and a plan, the awakening of a seed that contained the potential of all that is within it, an expression that sought expression. This stirring, this plan, this Word, was a germ within the unknown and it *was* the unknown.

---

[14] Compare with embryogenesis - the role of DNA, the process of mitosis and cell specialization

The Word stirred the unknown into activity, organizing a body around itself. And it gathered itself from the unknown, which was but its own self, growing and nourishing itself slowly, in an attempt to manifest the Master Plan it carried within. Soon a momentous time of Creation was at hand, for its body cleaved in two - its first real creation, an emanation of itself from itself. When the One became two, the process held the potential to create the Many. And so it did. Each grew, drawing from the unknown and then cleaved in two, and the newly created ones did likewise, fragmenting themselves almost endlessly, until the entire unknown became an expression of the Word.

And they communed with one another, working like a unity, but were actually a *trinity*, forming three groups of organization around a great Void. And this was the beginning of the next phase, that of diversity and manifestation. Each individual was an echo of the original One, and now each sought to manifest a different aspect of the One as directed by the Word within, becoming creators in their own right. One group became aspects of the Word that handled the creation of form and function. Another group dealt with the sustenance and nourishment of those forms. The third group dealt with intelligence, order and direction of that creation.

The first group dealt with *manifestation*, of form and function. It further specialized into sub-groups, some of which became supportive structures, the playing fields of life, the numerous terrains and levels where the plan within the Word could be manifested. Others became motive factors that manipulated the supportive structures, giving rise to a potential for movement and activity. Yet another sub-group became the life-blood that streamed through these groups, energizing them into activity.

The second major group dealt with the *sustenance* of this manifestation. Its sub-groups breathed life continuously into the Creation, assimilated nourishment and removed those elements that were found unsuitable to the Master Plan.

The third major group dealt with the *control and direction* of the manifestation. It organized itself into the Supreme Intelligence that functioned at the highest terrain or level of the Creation, from where it controlled and directed the rest of its body, organizing its goals and purposes. Its sub-groups merged into the manifestation as controlling factors, monitoring and directing most activity within it, setting up autonomous laws. Yet another sub-group came together and took on the task of beautifying the appearance of the Creation, masking its complexity.

And all the groups worked with one another, fulfilling the Great Master Plan resident within each, though the majority of the innumerable members that formed the Whole had little conception about the complexity of the whole as such, or about the greater order of which they were a part. (14)

The quickening happened at about six months, the tying of an arriving soul to the little body. Aliyah felt it as sudden and forceful movements within the womb. She called out excitedly, "Honey, the baby's moving!"

Theo came rushing, smiling broadly. She held his hands and placed them over her belly, guiding them so he could feel the baby's movement.

"I'll bet that's a boy, the way he's kicking!" grinned Theo.

"You are still hoping she's a boy, aren't you? That's not what the ultrasound indicated."

"Well, they make mistakes. You never know, y'know…"

Aliyah and Theo had been married for over two years. During this time she had been pleasantly surprised to find in him a great strength of character and a steely determination which had the ability to blaze new trails. But this nature of Theo also often expressed itself in a kind of rebellion against anything that imposed limitations or laws on his person. He loved to run free, uninhibited and unencumbered. And his passion and determination had made him successful, driven by goals and detailed planning. Unlike Aliyah, he still considered most of religion, spirituality and "other perversions" as opium to the masses. For him, they constituted a marketplace where different kinds of dubious goods were being manufactured and sold. This marketplace was to his utter distaste, which he considered grossly incompatible with the higher ideals professed by its vendors. And he had no qualms in stating his opinion whenever he pleased. In many ways, his beliefs were the antithesis of Aliyah's own. Perhaps she had hoped to change this and tame what she considered the untamable.

Theo had found himself drawn to Aliyah for many reasons. During their first meeting she had hit him right between the eyes. He had found himself thinking of her constantly, and therefore made many a pretext to get her attention and to talk with her. Besides her beauty, and the vibrant and caring nature, she exuded a strange quality, a vibration of some sort that held him captive. He could not explain it, but his own thoughts and feelings took higher ground when she was near, moving away from his usual thinking patterns to something more sublime. Her notions and expressions were far removed from what he had been accustomed to all his life, and the pull of the unknown was indeed fascinating. He could never have envisioned himself bonding with someone who professed a personal religion or God, as she did. But somehow their relationship had turned into a beautiful blossom which neither could explain to satisfaction.

"A baby has so much to teach us!" Aliyah sighed. "The miracle of creation! Isn't that wonderful?"

"Uh-oh! There's that gleam in your eye. I can see where this is heading…" laughed Theo.

"Sure, a baby is indeed a miracle of sorts," he continued, "but then so is our physiology, how the body and intelligence functions. What you call a miracle is but complex biological processes that we have not fully understood yet. You know what they say: any highly developed technology is indistinguishable from magic."

"You really don't think the baby is a miracle, do you?" Her voice had a hint of sadness.

"Aliyah, we are nature's products, using technology it gained through evolution. You too have recognized its technology many times. So there."

"But honey! How can you be so clinical and detached about the baby? Isn't she just adorable? An expression of ourselves? Creation in one of its highest forms?"

"Sure he is, sure he is," Theo grinned as he picked up a book. "Look, I'm reading this book on baby care. There's this narrative on the formative stages of the embryo, quite clinical and descriptive. I guess it's rubbing off on me!"

"I'm sure you will see the great miracle of creation there if you study it more closely," said Aliyah. "Unfortunately I have neither the time nor the patience for that exercise. With our baby coming, I find little interest in such stuff."

Theo was not to be put off. He opened the book, leafed through some of the pages and held it for her to see. He had his point to make.

"Look. Here's the fertilized ovum they call a zygote," he said. "It divides itself many times and starts looking like a ball they call a blastocyst. It appears to be a collection of cells formed around a central, fluid-filled cavity. Now look at this picture: it has developed some form. There are three major developments to be seen, the ectoderm, endoderm and the mesoderm, with an amniotic cavity inside. A trinity indeed, if I may borrow one of your favorite terms! The mesoderm develops into bones, muscles and connective tissues. The endoderm forms the digestive system, parts of the respiratory system and others. The ectoderm gives rise to the brain, spinal cord and nerves." [15]

"All right. Leave it now. I've had enough." Hormonal changes and her expected motherhood had started rubbing off on her priorities, and she found herself less interested in such discussions.

"Wait. Now here are some glimmerings of some recognizable shape. Look, the embryo baby now has a tail! This is nothing short of technological magic! It is DNA in each cell that carries the Master Plan of the body. God surely wouldn't need to create in such a fashion, would he?"

"Honey, what if that process itself is a reflection of how the Godhead externalized and expressed itself? Something tells me

---

[15] Compare with the first section of this chapter

there is more to that process than your matter-of-fact description of it."

"You go ponder about it!" laughed Theo. "I have to read through all this and more for the parenting classes. Well, you could try working these diapers on the dolly while you're at it. Gee, I can see this is going to be fun!"

Aliyah grimaced and lay back on the couch. A baby was a very exciting turn of events for her. From the loner and self-oriented person she used to be, she had come to share her life with Theo and now a baby was coming in, further expanding her love circle. She loved the baby even before it was born. The feeling of motherhood, its greatness, holiness and love, had already begun washing its sweeping tides over her. It was unlike anything she had ever felt before.

Her thoughts now turned to Theo, who somehow had a different frame of mind about the whole thing. She had met with little success in changing his opinions and his general outlook on life. Sometimes this drove her into despair, for the ideal world she pictured with Theo consistently failed to materialize. Worst of all was his rejection of the principles and truths that she held as sacred. But she suspected that deep down they had made a considerable impact, something that he refused to acknowledge or even consider. His materialistic viewpoint on life had often conflicted with hers, and she sometimes wondered how Theo had come into her life at all!

She remembered another time when she had described the body as holy and an image of God. There was the stomach, which represented earthly life, where digestion and assimilation took place, analogous to experiencing and learning. Above it were the protected higher worlds represented by the rib cage, where the heart and lungs were located. This she described as the higher worlds of love and life, for the heart was symbolically considered the seat of love, and the lungs provided the breath of life, and this area of the body circulated energies that helped sustain the whole body. Below the earthly domain represented by the stomach were to be found the intestines which represented lower worlds, purgatories or hells as they were called. Here too, amid the filth and stench, redemptive digestive assimilation occurred in the body, and the worst of the worst, the undesirables, were finally purged and discarded.

At the highest level, rising above the seven vertebrae of the neck, was to be found the brain, which represented the Great Intelligence that controlled all of creation. This brain, with its two hemispheres and the hindbrain, had a multi-fold nature. Principal among its functions were the intuitive and artistic intelligence represented by the right hemisphere, the intellectual and analytical represented by the left hemisphere and the autonomous and automatic coordination and control represented by the hindbrain. This by analogy represented to her the Supreme Intelligence functioning in the roles of the feminine or Mother, and that of the masculine or Father, and also in the impersonal and automatic laws and functioning of creation that were studied by the scientific community. This Great Intelligence acted on all the levels of Creation, from the highest to the very lowest, as represented by the extension through the spinal cord and the nerves that proceeded from it, merging into the rest of the body. To her this analogy of the physical body represented a real truth about the Body of God itself, that man's physical body was made in the image of God.

By now she had come to consider all her analogies as resulting from manifestations of cosmic principles, which like golden threads were woven seamlessly into the tapestry of all physical and spiritual phenomena. These principles resulted in phenomena at multiple levels mirroring one another in various degrees. The organizing principle behind an ovum and embryogenesis, she suspected to be a reflection of that which resulted in the Godhead unfolding itself. Those behind the organization of the human body, she considered to be a reflection of the ones which were behind the expression and functioning of the Godhead. Those that were behind the anatomical organization of a spider seemed reflected in the organization of the mafia super-organism and also in the spirit forces of evil. All such organizing principles she viewed as having emerged from a single, unifying principle that she called *the God Principle*, a term she used often with Emma. It was this Principle that ultimately resulted in the mirroring of various phenomena at multiple levels and in subtle ways, and formed the basis for all the analogies that held her attention captive. The result was a great reflection of the physical and spiritual realms on to each other, and even within their own realms.

Theo however had found her descriptions somewhat incredulous, and a product of weird imagination. Such apparent insensitivity on his part and some ridicule of her cherished notions many times resulted in her moving into depression, resulting in emotional tantrums that flared up every now and then. These incidents caused Theo to move even further away from her ideals, as her tantrums were distasteful to him in the extreme. Despite such ideological differences, love kept them together. Indeed they were learning from each other in subtle ways, too subtle to be noticed over short periods of time.

For Aliyah was now entering a troublesome period in her life, one that was calculated to make her realize that spirituality had little to do with philosophies, theologies or even experiences of so-called spiritual states; that true spirituality had to do with how she lived, what she learned and how she responded within to everyday life.

14. Sea

Aliyah explores the human subconscious and its parallels in nature.

In the many months and years that followed, Aliyah and Theo experienced and understood the joys, struggles, frustrations and rewards of parenting, and also the love, commitment and sacrifice it took to sustain their family unit. The lessons came through significant emotional turmoil, with her outbursts often taxing Theo heavily. She was coming face to face with aspects of herself that she had never suspected existed. The sunny and bright surface of her emotional waters could quickly turn into a dark, roiling tempest on short notice. At times, Theo could trigger certain deep emotions in her by a simple spoken word, a careless action, a mocking gesture or even by his silence. She had no clue how these slights managed to push her buttons, except that they did. And she found herself plumbing the depths of a sea of emotion inside her being, only to discover that there was precious little she knew about her own nature. There was indeed a deep sea of unknown and uncharted territory within. And a sea it was, for she quickly recognized the association.

For the seas of the earth composed a proper reflection of human emotional nature. The sea drew people irresistibly to herself like a magnet, to sail her waters and to settle on her shores. With beautiful rolling waves and soothing rhythms, shimmering waters, cool winds, lapping tides, gorgeous sunrises and sunsets, and depths that cradled creatures both fascinating and mysterious, the sea always held human imagination captive. Like an enchantress she called to human souls with all her beauty and seductiveness, and like the sirens of old she could also be dangerous. The calm and cool reveries could quickly change into a tempest, with stormy winds under the darkened brow of the sky lashing up great waves, which tossed, turned, foamed, churned and lashed with unimaginable power and ferocity, swallowing many a ship or boat that got caught in her fury. At times she invaded the land and washed away whole towns and cities. The sea was often considered moody, fickle, even treacherous, and men tended to associate a feminine nature with the sea, signifying an overabundance of emotional natures. The loving, caring, peaceful and happy nature of positive emotions, and the horrendous destructive power of rampant negative emotions were blatantly displayed by the sea for all those who looked to see.

Did this curious association of the emotional with the sea go any deeper? Within the human body was also to be found another sea, that of blood. More than two-thirds of the earth was covered with oceans, and like its counterpart, the red sea within occupied more than two-thirds of the human body. The most common element dissolved in sea water was sodium chloride or common salt. The same element was abundantly present in the human red sea, making blood salty to the tongue. Oceanic currents moved nutrients and warmth throughout its own watery body and also through the atmosphere as the well known water cycle, enabling life to flourish on land and in the sea. The water cycle brought back from land dissolved filth and waste, and also minerals and nutrients that were recycled into its waters. These oceanic currents also moved warmth throughout the earth, often passing on the heat to the winds, bringing warmth to the continents. The red sea within the human body also had its currents, which moved nutrients and heat throughout the body and returned wastes for recycling or disposal. And the blood was esoterically considered the carrier of *emotional energy*, with the heart being the center from which the energies circulated. Indeed, the very terms hot-blooded and cold-blooded were often associated with an abundance and a lack of emotions, respectively, and it was a curious fact that warm-blooded animals generally seemed to show emotional responses that the cold-blooded variety lacked. The menstrual cycles of women tended to follow cycles similar to lunar cycles, during which they could become moody, depressed and irritable, much as the sea too had her high and low tides influenced by the moon. There seemed to exist a curious association between the sea - whether the internal red sea or the external blue oceans - and human emotional natures.

Yet the connections with the sea were even deeper. Her vast and unfathomable depths mirrored the subconscious and unconscious levels that existed within human beings. While the higher levels of the atmosphere mirrored the higher mind and the more refined emotional aspects of consciousness, the sea and its depths mirrored the primitive emotional and lower-mind aspect of consciousness. Indeed the atmosphere held large amounts of moisture in the form of water vapor, just as the ocean and its depths held large amounts of dissolved air that allowed species to thrive. The surface of the sea with its dancing waves, the winds above, and the thin photic zone that existed beneath the surface reflected the average human consciousness. The waves were created by winds that transferred their energy to the sea. These mirrored human thoughts that encouraged emotions, resulting in turbulence. Often these waves were beautiful and gentle, but it took only a few sustained, strong winds to whip them into a frenzy, upon which the sea literally roared. But this energy exchange was not always in one direction. The waters could store energy for prolonged periods of time, just as emotional energy remained latent within human beings for long periods of time. Winds fed off this energy of the sea and transformed into great hurricanes that blew in and devastated shores. The emotional energy latent within human beings was often expressed likewise, for it greatly encouraged thoughts that resulted in violent behavior. It seemed that the surface of the sea thus reflected the average human consciousness in a peculiar manner.

But consciousness also had a deeper side which was often expressed not in the waking state, but during sleep, such as in dreams played out by the subconscious. The dream world appeared to have a separate reality of its own, apart from waking reality, much like the sea existed separately from the land. Indeed, the oceans had terrains and ecosystems similar to those on land. There were mountains taller than Mt. Everest, canyons larger than Grand Canyon, forests such as those of giant kelp, and plains wider than the Serengeti. There were rivers and waterfalls of ocean currents, cold and barren deserts where little of life was to be found, oases of geysers or hydrothermal vents, fiery undersea volcanoes, deep chasms and caves, and even terrain that looked literally out of this world. Hypsographic analysis of the earth's crust revealed two independent bell-shaped curves for the continental and oceanic crusts, indicating that the domains of the land and the sea lived nearly separate lives that progressed on their own, yet had reflections of one another. Like waking and dreaming consciousness, the revealed and the hidden, day and night, the land and the sea existed side by side. Indeed, much of the seas were antipodal to land, positioned diametrically opposite land-masses on the globe, as the continent of Antarctica was antipodal to the Arctic sea. And like the ecosystems and creatures on land which carried reflections of his nature, the sea hinted at an alternate reality of the terrestrial dwelling human, that of his hidden nature in the form of his subconscious and the unconscious.

And how deep was this association? The surface of the sea, and the photic or light zone below represented the area of highest activity with the largest number of animals, where fish both large and small were to be found. This zone represented the average human consciousness where the mind and the emotions interacted. Going further down from the photic zone, the light faded and the active and dynamic movement characteristic of the upper layers was no longer to be found. There was an eerie ambience here, with its still, cold, lonely and dark waters, and the constant rain of organic matter drizzling down from upper layers. This level was particularly nutrient-rich, from which cold upswells brought much needed nutrients to upper levels where they fostered large-scale plankton blooms. These blooms were critical to the oceanic food-chain, as all life at those levels depended on these. Biological productivity, as the process was known, depended on this nutrient supply from deeper layers. Likewise the productivity of the average consciousness also depended on upswells from deeper layers. This level thus represented the deeper human subconscious, from which often welled-up useful concepts, ideas and solutions which were then processed by the average consciousness. More interestingly, the subconscious was usually more productive after the conscious mind had worked on a concept, applied straining thoughts to it. Likewise plankton blooms and increased biological productivity were usually found to follow a typical storm, after the winds helped stir up the deep waters and bring nutrients to the surface.

But this level had to do with more than nutrient supply to higher levels. While there were fewer fish and other animals to be found at these depths, there were much larger species, like the giant squids, great white sharks and the whales that dove down into these deeper layers. This was also the supposed lair of the mysterious animals that formed sailors' mythological lore across many seas and historical times. These included the leviathan, kraken or the sea serpent, selkies, sirens, mermaids and mermen, and many other sea creatures both curious and fantastic. These conceptual species represented mythological and primitive fears and fascinations that existed within, subconscious complexes that surfaced now and then, which where projected into both inspirations and phobias.

Going down further deep, there was total darkness, and the pressure of the water column became enormously great. Here were to be found the strangest, most bizarre and bestial creatures of the deep, many of whose very visages appeared literally devilish, such as the viperfish and the ogrefish. This was indeed a strange world with creatures unlike anything seen at higher levels. This layer represented the depths of the unconscious, the realm of the primordial and archetypal complexes that existed deep within the human consciousness and also in the collective unconscious of the race. Those who had come in contact with complexes at these levels were often haunted by the nature of emotions they brought about, which could twist the personality into a deranged mentality, exhibiting extreme forms of behavior. To this ocean level ultimately rained down all the refuse and unwanted material from the lighter depths, from mineral, silt and sewage runoffs taken from land by the rivers, biological matter from upper layers, to sunken ships and whale carcasses. The unconscious likewise contained a great accumulation of decayed past experiences accumulated throughout the eons, primarily of an unwanted and negative kind. From there, it influenced the subconscious and conscious levels in subtle ways.

And yet the unconscious held more than strange or terrifying complexes symbolized by these creatures of the deep. These levels were closest to the mantle and thus the core of the earth, the primordial center which represented the body of God from which emanated the evolving consciousness. The heat and the volcanic action at the bottom level warmed the oceans and helped keep their chemical content in balance for life to survive and proliferate on the planet. A process of subduction continuously recycled, albeit slowly, the ocean bed, returning unwanted accumulation into the body of the earth in subduction zones, with new material projected forth in volcanic zones. The sea floor continuously spread. Likewise, the waste and refuse of the deeper layers of the unconscious were also subject to recycling, purification and re-projection through the body of God. And moving from the oceanic crust, through the waters, into the atmosphere and towards the Sun was to be found again the progression through the four elements of earth, water, wind and fire, representing the drive from the physical or the state of existence and pure being, to the emotional, to the mental and to the spiritual realms, the highest level of becoming. The layers from the deep earth to the Sun thus represented a progression from being to becoming and beyond, two opposite ends of the great spectrum of the unfolding manifestation of the Godhead.

The same was reflected even at the planetary level, when moving from Earth which represented physical existence, past Venus which represented love or emotions, and past Mercury which represented mind, to reach the Sun which represented spirit.[16] Between Earth and Venus one crossed the orbit of the moon which too represented the subconscious and the unconscious, much like the depths of the sea. For the effect of the moon on the human consciousness was known well to law enforcement and hospital workers, that of triggering heightened violence, abnormal behavior and even lunacy during full moon and new moon days. Even the very term moon-struck was part of common lore. Thus the association between the moon and the sea had deeper significance, for the subconscious and the deep-seated unconscious represented the remnants of earlier stages of becoming, one which was meant to be transcended for ascension into higher levels. And this ascension meant rising above their influences, past the higher mind into pure spirit.

Aliyah recognized the sea within and directed her energies as best as she could towards taming its uncontrolled nature. Her roiling emotional tempests started mellowing considerably. She was now much more aware and mature, in control of herself and able to resist the pull of wayward emotions. Theo, though harsh at times, had taught her how to exercise and channel her own will into directing the tremendous emotional energy latent within. This was now reflected in her social work with children. Mind, *the builder*, had reigned in her thoughts and emotions and helped manifest

---

[16] These are primarily astrological associations

that emotional energy constructively, channeled into practical activities. Her river no longer ran where and how the terrain dictated, and its floodwaters no longer posed a threat to anyone. The dams, the aqueducts and other systems that harnessed the river now spread its vibrant life and energy constructively into a large area. The waters gave of itself to everything that it touched, and life abounded in its wake. All her self-seeking, questions and confusions disappeared. She focused more and more on daily life, fulfilling what she considered her sacred duty to her family, to her society, to her nation, to humanity, and to her God. And her river went forth merrily on its journey to the sea.

Life soon found Aliyah on the beach by the ocean, where the physical, mental, emotional and spiritual met and united in peace and harmony. The sun-bleached sands lapped by shimmering waves and caressed by bracing winds ceaselessly called out to humanity for recognition. Here the four elements came together and blended with one another exquisitely, offering a deep reflection of what human beings always sought within. And hearing the great call, they always came by the millions, as numerous as the grains of sand upon the seashore, to bask in peace and tranquility, to swim, to play and to have fun, and to gaze in wonder at the beautiful countenance of the solar orb that bathed them in its glory.

Finally Aliyah had found herself.

15. Chaos

Aliyah explains the mission of Christ and more from natural laws.

The door creaked open and a flash of light streamed through, illuminating dusty tables, chairs, old lamps and other furniture. The beam paused briefly to survey a derelict painting on the wall, now covered with cobwebs and caked with dirt. A young man adorned in what appeared to be the finest clothes of a bygone era, and brandishing a sword, stared back at the intruder from its depths. The beam moved on again over the walls, revealing spiders and other insects that scurried away to apparent safety, and it came down to rest upon an old chest in one corner of the room, partly hidden away by a tapestry that appeared faded and discolored. A faint light seeped in through gaps and cracks in the window sills, painting a still life picture wrought of shadows.

The door opened wider and the intruder stepped into the room.

"Wow! This place is ancient! Look at everything covered with dust. And cobwebs too… What happened to this room?"

"No one's been in here for quite a while, Eloise," replied Aliyah, following in after her daughter. "This is what happens when things are left all to themselves, unattended."

"Okay, so where is it then? The great picture you said you're going to show me? Is it the one there on the wall? I don't think so. Perhaps it's stashed away in that big chest over there?"

"Patience, Eloise!" Aliyah coughed as she struggled with a window and finally managed to open it. A shaft of sunlight streamed through and hit the floors, illuminating the rest of the room. Particles of dust swirled.

"There are two great movements of matter that you can easily discern everywhere, Eloise. One is that of life, of order. It is a movement of creativity, growth and expansion. Look over at that tree out there." Aliyah pointed outside.

"The other great movement is that of dissipation, disorder, chaos. And that is what you see prominent in here. These two great movements are like natural laws. Their manifestations are everywhere," she continued.

"Thanks for the lecture, Mom!" Eloise walked over to the wooden chest in the corner and swept away its cobwebs with a piece of wood she found on the floor. She was now very curious, and nothing else in the room attracted her attention as much. She dusted the chest a little and after a bit of fumbling, lifted up the heavy lid which creaked and swung up on a hinge. Her flashlight soon explored its contents.

"Aha, so *this* is your treasure!" Eloise exclaimed as she looked into the chest. "And it doesn't smell too bad, after all these years! Sandalwood, is it?"

Aliyah said nothing and watched Eloise dig into the chest.

"Clothes, looks more like costumes… a bunch of old letters… small bottles… of perfume? … wooden tigers and elephants… turban… a dagger! … books… ooh what's this?" Eloise exclaimed. "I'll bet this is the one!"

She pulled out a large article wrapped carefully in ornate cloth. Excitedly, she unwrapped the package and held it to the light streaming from the window. The light revealed an old black and white photograph of a family seated in regalia in a British colonial setting.

"Looks like this item managed to keep your law of disorder at bay, Mom." She exclaimed as she inspected the picture. "Now look at her! She looks just like you!"

"Yes Eloise, that is my grandmother. It's a strong likeness, isn't it?" Aliyah moved closer to inspect the picture. "And the little lady there who resembles you is my mother, your grandmother, that is. You know she died giving me life. Behind her next to my grandma is Granddad. If you look, there are three generations of the family here…" her voice trailed off.

Eloise studied the picture. She had heard some detail once in a while, but the information was scanty and she hadn't been very interested anyway. Now the picture took on a special meaning as she contemplated her family tree and life as it would have been, generations ago.

Then something caught her eye.

"Look at all the stuff around them! And those people, were those…?"

"Servants, yes. In colonial times the family was indeed rich. My great granddad was born soon after his dad was posted there on official business. Within a lifetime they acquired large estates. Now all that is gone. We manage with what we have here."

"But isn't that country poor, Mom? Why would they choose to live there?"

"I am not sure, Eloise. It is said that it was very rich once, and then all that was taken away. There is a letter from my grandfather on the matter somewhere in here. You know, he was something of a philanthropist. And he was into studying their religion and philosophy. Now he did have some interesting views…"

Aliyah picked up a bunch of letters, thumbed through them and finally pulled out one. "Here it is, now be careful with it!"

167

Brown at the edges and somewhat wizened with age, the papers and the scribbles on it bespoke a vanished time and culture. Excitement was plain on her countenance as Eloise held it in her hands. However, she couldn't make much sense of their contents and puzzlement appeared on her face. But she looked at them for a long while.

"Here, let me read out some of it for you." Aliyah gently took the papers from Eloise. "Now be aware that the way he writes, meaning his style, is a little different from what we are accustomed to."

She proceeded to carefully scan the letter and then read out loud:

> *"To this country was once gifted the high truths, very long ago, which are to be found in her sages of old, their teachings and their writings. They wrote the great truths within their hearts and minds, and taught her kings and her commoners.*
>
> *But what she made of that great inheritance was to oppress her fellow man, create castes and creeds, and practically enslave those who were always meant to be equal and free. And did she all this in the name of truth.*
>
> *With the gift of higher truth also comes great responsibility. When higher truth is misused, the punishment is even heavier. She was in turn enslaved to a conquering nation, and found herself ground under its heel, even as she oppressed her own supposedly lower castes. Her glory was taken away, and she found herself in a veritable desert of body and spirit, haunted by ghosts of charlatans and recurring mirages, her spiritual oases few and far between. Such is the power of the great law of retribution at work in her being, for she reaps only*

what she herself did sow, and reap she does, many
times over."

"Is that true mom?" Eloise whispered, "Were there slaves
there?"

"Not in the letter of the word Eloise, but in its spirit I
think. There were and still are many castes and other divisions
there. He is talking about those who were called the lower
castes."

Aliyah continued reading:

> *"But all is not lost, for in her are still to be found*
> *the seedlings of that great fount of wisdom and truth,*
> *if one but searches among the weeds that now litter*
> *her vanished orchards. And when she has paid for*
> *her mistakes to the utmost farthing, they will raise*
> *her up once again to her past glory, with a great*
> *wisdom of life unequalled by any other nation*
> *anytime in history. But her path upward appears*
> *long and arduous, perchance strewn with blood and*
> *littered with bodies.*
>
> *Weep for this nation, o man! For hers is a great*
> *burden, a horrendous debt-of-law that keeps her in*
> *poverty and misery.*
>
> *Pray for this nation, o man! For there is much*
> *more she has to endure before her sun truly rises."*

Aliyah stopped reading and looked up.

"Whew! I can see where you got your genes, Mom!" Eloise
exclaimed.

Then she was thoughtful. "I sure hope he was wrong. He
mentioned a law of retribution, and of sowing and reaping.
Are there such things?"

"Yes, Eloise. The law of sowing and reaping, the law of
retribution, the law of consequences, all are varied ways of
expressing the same principle. But if you ask me, behind them

is a great law of acceleration. It is the same that is expressed behind the two great movements I was telling you about, that of chaos and that of order."

"Acceleration of what, Mom?" asked Eloise as she took the letter from her mother.

"Of everything, Eloise! In the so-called natural world, growth is an acceleration, and so is death or dissipation, which is also an acceleration in the reverse direction."

"But I don't see any acceleration," said Eloise. "How come?"

"You have to look carefully. A lot of what you see in life is a balance of forces between these two great movements, at work against each other. Your body cells are dying, but they are being replenished with new ones. An office room gets dusty but is being swept clean every day, and the walls are coated with new paint once in a while. You can see that both movements are at work in a well-maintained system, resulting in an apparent status quo or stasis."

"So where is the acceleration, Mom?"

"In a minute, Eloise. You need to understand the movement of life that you see in the natural world. There is a thrust, or an acceleration of growth, which is usually followed by a period of active stasis where the forces more or less balance one another, and then at some point the active thrusting force of growth often wears out and acceleration in the reverse direction gets the upper hand. The end result is death."

'Mom, come to the point! Why do you use the term acceleration?"

"What does a force do in the natural world, Eloise? You have studied many laws of physics, including Newton's laws. Application of force on an object results in its acceleration. The very definition of force in physics includes a key component called acceleration, a multiplication factor. It is then a fundamental law of nature, is it not? Only when forces balance, is uniform motion or stillness possible. Otherwise acceleration is the rule."

"You're talking too abstract, Mom," complained Eloise as she folded the papers and placed the letter back among its sisters, tying them up again into a neat bunch.

"Is it difficult to see that growth is also an acceleration? Consider this, then. Why do we farm? How many times more grain do you get than when you sow? Ten times? Twenty? Forty? If that is not acceleration, a multiplication factor, what is it then?"

"Okay, Mom. But why do you say that dissipation is acceleration too?"

"Well, has anyone ever farmed and come up with the same amount of grain as that which was sown? That would indeed be a rare occurrence. Either you reap much more than you sow, or you lose most of it due to natural factors like pests, diseases, floods and infertile soil. Try sowing on rock, for instance. The way natural processes work, you may gain much more than you put in or, on the other hand, lose what little you have."

Eloise still looked a little puzzled.

Aliyah continued, "All right. Imagine that you are an oak seedling growing in a small clearing in the woods, along with scores of other seedlings. What are the chances of your survival? It depends on the amount of sunlight you can reach. It is a race to the top, as to who can grow tall enough and fast enough to reach the canopy. The clearing will soon disappear, covered by foliage of the new trees, and the seedlings that do not grow well for whatever reasons, or those that come later, will not get sufficient sunlight. They will lose whatever little sunlight they get and thus die. Haven't you read in the scriptures? To those who have, more will be given. To those who have not, even what little they have will be taken away. It is indeed an acceleration, in either direction."

"Mom, that's really scary! You are saying it is a spiritual law as well? Is there no justice?"

"A gardener would not plant his garden that way, would he, Eloise?" Aliyah asked pointedly.

"You mean there is a gardener in the spirit, Mom?"

171

"Good question, Eloise. I will let you ponder that. But remember that a gardener or a farmer only directs the growth and dissipation processes inherent in nature. Like careful planting, watering, fertilizers, pruning, weeding, placing of obstacles that break up winds, controlling light and shade, and so on. Despite all that, life in a garden, orchard or farm proceeds by natural laws and processes. A gardener cannot do much about them."

"I don't understand, Mom. What can't he do?"

"Consider an orchard, Eloise. If its plants have developed serious defects that make them prone to disease, the orchard may not survive. The grower may have no choice but to remove diseased plants if they cannot be healed, especially if they threaten the health of the whole orchard. Those removed plants will inevitably rot and disappear through the action of natural dissipative agents. Well, the plants are not really lost, as their essence will be recycled through the body of the earth. But you will never see one as a single plant again. Their identities are lost forever."

"Mom, are you speaking in metaphors?"

"Indeed they are spiritual metaphors, Eloise. You can take it further. A plant not tended by a gardener grows wild, at the mercy of natural processes that may help it grow as well as die. If it is on the path of growth, it will multiply and bring forth many saplings. Or it may regress and die helplessly. Many souls of our human life stream have willed themselves away from the care of a Gardener, care which is available for the asking. They have literally grown wild and many have fallen victims to natural forces that drag them towards dissipation. This happens because human souls have what may be called a free will."

"Mom, it doesn't sound like justice to me, to allow souls to regress and dissipate, even be recycled, like you say."

"Eloise, it is the highest form of freedom if you but understand it. So let us try to do so, first in terms of pure physics. Remember what we discussed earlier? Any force acting on any object results in an acceleration of the object in the direction of the applied force. There can of course be a multitude of forces in different directions acting on the object, and the movement of the object happens in the direction of the composite force."

"I know that, Mom. That's pretty much trivial."

"Is it really? Then look at the higher or spiritual version of the same law. It states that every action through intent, by any being, in any chosen direction, is accelerated by the spiritual universe. That is to say, if you choose to do good, then it becomes easier and easier to do greater good. And if you choose to do evil, it becomes easier and easier to do greater evil. And by corollary, it becomes even more difficult to go the other way, that is, to switch directions."

"I guess I can relate to that. Once habits are ingrained it is difficult to change tracks, isn't it?"

"It is more than habits, Eloise, it is about life itself, and about a soul's progress over great spans of time. For example, if you continually choose to ignore wisdom when it is given, then it becomes more and more difficult later to understand the same when it is given to you. In fact, it becomes difficult to even come across true wisdom. It is thus a very powerful law of acceleration. It always furthers one's choices, whether the choices are good, bad or neutral in human terms. It is behind the effect of sowing and reaping. The reaping in spiritual terms is many times more than that which was sown."

Eloise was silent. Perhaps it was true, she reflected. But was it just? she asked herself.

"It is indeed fair, Eloise!" Aliyah said, as though in response to her thoughts. "The universe lets you choose and then it furthers your choice, in whatever direction your choice may be. But every choice has its consequences. And when you make many choices, there is always a composite that results. The composite pattern may or may not be to your liking, but it is nevertheless built from your choices and their consequences."

"Mom, I don't often see sowing and reaping happening as you say. People go on with their lives. Fortunes or misfortunes come out of the blue, as though by mere chance."

"How long should a farmer wait for oranges after he has planted his seedlings in the ground? The result is not

173

instantaneous, not a few days, not even months. There is a matter of time there, often many years, when natural processes at work ultimately bring forth fruit, many times over. Likewise the higher laws work over timescales of the soul, and the results often seem to come out of the blue, and also are magnified. Do they not say that when troubles come they seem to come together, and everything seems to go wrong? The personality may not understand the timing or the effects, but the soul or higher self does."

"It does sound logical, Mom. But I still have difficulty believing that souls could be, what shall I say, lost?"

"Isn't that what nature teaches you? The loss is in a soul's identity, Eloise, or its organization, if you will. The soul stuff is not really lost. But there are dissipative agents at work that cause a progressive breakdown of its organization. Look closely at that chair over there and tell me what you see."

Eloise looked where Aliyah pointed, and in a moment she understood.

"Termites! That chair is being eaten away!"

"Indeed! There are many orders of life that thrive on a degenerating soul, using up its energies at many possible levels before its identity is fully dissipated. I do not wish to discuss it, but you can find out for yourself by studying that pattern in nature."

"Mom, you are scaring me! Are there many such souls?"

"Eloise, can you imagine the human life stream with its billions of souls? Now think of the great law of acceleration working on these individual souls, furthering their choices. And then again think of the two great movements of life, one towards greater order and the other towards chaos. You can see that there is exerted a great pressure on the unity of our life stream, forcing it in different directions, or two primary directions, if you will, because of individual choices. What do you think will happen?"

"The life-stream will splinter?"

"Indeed, it has no choice but to splinter sometime or other. A portion will regress and disappear, and the rest will progress.

It is inevitable, Eloise. Haven't you heard? One will be taken and the other left behind. That phrase is but an expression of the law of acceleration, the inexorable result of our own choices, as individuals and as a life-stream."

"Mom, can't something be done about it? If what you say is true, all humanity is one, and those who fall back are but ourselves, aren't they?"

Eloise had touched on a matter so terribly important, yet so universally ignored.

"Truly, Eloise! Truly! And there did come a time in the past when our life stream was about to crack in two. And something was indeed done about it."

"What, Mom, what?" asked Eloise excitedly.

"It is history, Eloise. It is well known that a great being stood in the gap, took the infirmities of our life stream upon Himself and gave many of us another chance. He propitiated the great law of retribution and held the life stream together."

Eloise was silent in contemplation. Aliyah watched her intently for a while.

"It is not difficult to identify Him, Eloise. For His symbol is that same great cross-road that the race is gazing at again today. His blood was shed on it once, but it cannot save the race forever."

Presently Eloise broke her silence.

"Mom, then there is no permanent solution?"

"Unfortunately not, Eloise. Not as long as free will exists. In human terms, it is really sad. It is inevitable that many shall regress, a result of our own choices. We can only work and hope that our fragment that chooses to regress is as small as possible. That is the great burden of soul for many, many people who are now working for humanity. They do not understand it quite in the same terms as you do now, but that does not really matter, does it? The burden of their hearts is the same. It would be very much like me losing you forever."

Aliyah had tears in her eyes as she embraced her daughter and held her tight.

"You see, dearest, the great picture that I promised to show you is not a photograph, nor the contents of this chest. It is but this room itself and the great panorama of higher life that it helps paint for you. Always choose the light, dear Eloise, and strive to lighten the burden of your brethren, for they are but yourself. And never forget that nature shows all, tells all. Sometimes her stories are sad, but necessarily so."

The door closed behind them and darkness pervaded the room. The relentless forces of chaos were again back to work.

16. War

Aliyah on war, the Mahabharata, and the forgiveness of sins.

"The madness of war!", exclaimed Eloise, gazing at the endless rows of gravestones and crosses that stretched from where she stood, seemingly all the way into infinity. "How can it even exist in a spiritual universe? Yet many religious scriptures are steeped in war!"

Eloise had attended a candlelight vigil the previous day, on the anniversary of an act of war on her country. She had found herself highly emotional throughout its proceedings, and greatly perplexed as to the logic of it all. A subsequent visit to the national memorial cemetery did nothing to improve her morale.

"Some say it has to do with the so-called eternal conflict between good and evil," replied Emma, taking her hand.

"Scriptures use them as illustrations to tell you what you should and not do."

Emma still frequented Aliyah's family, and had even become a mentor to the young girl.

"Yeah? Well, some of those illustrations are simply disgusting! Read them and you wonder why people consider them holy scripture at all! Don't you think a lot of evil in the world has come from religions?" Eloise questioned.

"Shh!" admonished Emma.

Aliyah placed her offering of roses in front of the grave. The white tombstone had a name etched on it, which was slowly fading from the onslaught of the elements through the many years it had stood there. She hung her head, whispered a prayer and stood in silence for a while. Sunlight poured through the trees and reflected on her hair, highlighting streaks of grey and white amid lush tresses. Then she turned away slowly from her father's grave.

Aliyah walked towards Eloise, gathered her in her arms and the pair retraced their steps towards the chapel, followed by Emma close behind. They walked in silence till Emma caught up with them. Then Aliyah said in a low tone,

"I heard your question, Eloise!"

"I'm sorry, Mom! I couldn't help it!"

"That's okay," Aliyah smiled, "perhaps we can talk about some of your questions on scriptures and war."

"You will? I mean, why religions cause war and all that?"

Aliyah paused for a moment, considering her daughter.

"Scriptures are accelerators of what we carry within, Eloise, like the acceleration we talked about before!" she said gently. "They provide an impetus for many natures within us to develop faster, those seeds of what you might call good and evil."

"Oh, they are not promoting only good? I thought they were supposed to!"

"Well, I am going to be really *melodramatic* here! What you'd call the forces of good and evil, or of order and chaos, they have equal rights. Otherwise it wouldn't be fair, would it?"

"Fair? Why should it be fair towards evil? Why can't everything be of the light?"

"Well, one of the reasons for us to be here is to discover ourselves and our natures! Without expressing, understanding and even cleansing many of those, a soul cannot make progress. But how can we even discover and cleanse negative impressions if there is no opportunity?"

Eloise did not respond.

"Scriptures help express many of our natures, by accelerating their development. A lot of good and a lot of evil that we see in history are a result of that acceleration. It's not the scriptures that are at fault; we are simply meeting ourselves."

"I thought scriptures were meant for our edification!"

"They serve that purpose, yes. But the same scripture which provides inspiration to those who seek higher wisdom, can also feed a religious fanatic and a rabid terrorist. Many viewpoints you carry can be accelerated by scriptures. If you prefer to go lower, that is available. Any time you are ready for a higher viewpoint, the selfsame scripture can also show you the way."

"Mom, that may be! But there are plenty of scriptures that talk about the wrath of God, how He curses people and takes revenge. You see so much of bloodshed and cruelty in these stories. And the same thing happens in the world today. Surely God cannot be like that?"

"Does that really bother you?"

"You bet it does! I think any rational person would wonder about it!"

"But there are millions who find it perfectly acceptable!"

"I don't understand it, Mom! They may find it acceptable, but not me! God cannot be wrathful, jealous and punishing!"

"Eloise, both viewpoints are correct, yours as well as theirs!" said Aliyah, as they approached the chapel.

"Mom! What are you saying? The two are like night and day. How can both be right? That would be incredible!"

"Really? That's because truth is *beyond* good and evil. Our perception of truth makes us see it in one of many ways, as good or evil in some cases."

"Well, maybe, Mom! But you haven't answered my question. How can both be true?"

Aliyah studied her daughter silently for a moment.

"Eloise, it's not difficult to understand at all. I did tell you about the law of retribution, of sowing and reaping, didn't I?"

"Yes."

"Do you have complaints about that impersonal law of justice?"

"No Mom! It makes more sense than a vengeful and jealous God! You have also said that it is a force that brings us progressively closer to the Godhead."

"See? Many of us think of these laws as impersonal and we have no problems with it. But we need not always consider them as impersonal."

"What do you mean, Mom?"

"If you had a personal relationship with what you consider as the Godhead, how might this law be expressed *in that relationship?*"

"I don't understand, Mom!"

"What I mean is that the laws can also become personified when you establish a personal relationship with the Godhead. The laws are then expressed, depending on the *nature* of the relationship!"

"You mean the laws become a person?"

"Well, the laws are not separate from the Godhead. When expressed in a relationship, a law *could* find expression *personally* as 'I will destroy your wives and your children and I will give your land to an invader, unless you turn away from your ways!'"

"Such messages always came through prophets," continued Aliyah, "who had their own relationship with the Godhead. Their experiences were dependent on the nature of their relationship, and intensely personified. The expressions of the laws then became prophetic warnings of doom and disaster, and of a wrathful and jealous God."

"You mean they were wrong in their perception, Mom?"

"I didn't say that, Eloise! Only that both viewpoints are correct. You must learn to make your own choices! Now let's sit down here for a minute."

They settled down on the neatly trimmed lawn in front of the chapel. Eloise regarded her mother curiously and considered this new viewpoint. It seemed to have some validity, as she could view the laws as impersonal or personal, depending on her preference.

"Maybe you have a point, Mom!" she replied thoughtfully. "But I still find it difficult to see anything good in any scripture that is peppered with bloodshed and war!"

"It depends on what you observe," replied Aliyah. "A scriptural story of bloodshed and war can have higher meanings beyond the literal reading."

"Oh, really? Then show me even one scripture where bloodshed and war can mean anything higher!"

"I can relate to that!" intervened Emma, who had been silent throughout the exchange. "There is this great epic of the far east which I have been reading. It is the story of a great war.[17] It is considered scripture by millions. What you just mentioned, about a higher point of view in a war story, just came to mind."

"Which story is that, Emma?" Eloise seemed curious.

"Well, it's the story of five princes[18] and their war. The war is with their cousins[19] and their armies. I'm sure you've heard about it."

"Yes, I've read about it long ago," replied Eloise. "What did you find in it?"

"Well, one might pass it off as a great novel with all the twists and turns, though it is supposed to be based on history.

---

[17] The *Mahabharata*
[18] The Pandavas
[19] The Kauravas

But soon you realize that the author is not biased the way many historians are. Even though the story is commonly regarded as the triumph of good over evil, the good people in it are not absolutely good and the evil are not absolutely evil. The armies even stop fighting every evening and warriors visit each other. This made me think."

"You mean they are all symbolic?" asked Eloise.

It was Aliyah who answered, "You know, Eloise, most scriptures are masterpieces of penmanship. They have multiple meanings, not just the symbolic. But I guess Emma is referring to a symbolic aspect of the story."

"Yes!" said Emma as she made a face, "Though I wouldn't have quite put it that way!"

"Okay, then, tell us what you found as a higher viewpoint in a war story!" said Eloise.

"Well," began Emma, "your mother continues to have a curious influence on me! So much so that I have even looked into the so-called science of the planets. Are you familiar with it?"

"You mean how planets *don't* control us, but function more like a clock or calendar that we look up? [20] Yes, Mom told me about that!"

"Then you won't be scared off if I mention Mercury, Mars, Jupiter and so on?"

"No! I am aware of how people *mistakenly* think that these planets affect their lives."

"Great! Now did you also know that the ancients associated the human hand with these planets, too?"

"No! Why would they?"

"Well," remarked Aliyah, "the hand is our primary means of action in the world. Just like the planets were used to describe a calendar of lessons and tests in life, it made sense to them to use the hand too."

"You mean symbolically, like the planets?"

---

[20] See chapter 'Rhythm'

"Yes." This from Emma. "The five fingers represent five major lessons and tests we must face in life. The ancients considered each finger as associated with a planet, and representing a major lesson and a major test in life."

"I see, so those five princes correspond to the five fingers? The war story corresponds to the lessons and tests in life?"

"There you are! The curious part is how the story makes no direct mention of this. But it's there if you look!"

"Well, then tell me about the princes!" Eloise settled down and looked at Emma in anticipation.

"All right, then!" Emma laughed. "Let's start in order, with the thumb. What do you see special about it?"

"Well, it is stronger for sure, compared to the others."

"Yes, it is the strongest and thickest finger on the hand, and symbolic of strength, power and aggression. It is supposedly ruled by Mars, associated with aggression and war. Mars represents aggressive energy, pure and simple."

"Okay, so one of the princes is like that?"

"Yes," agreed Emma, "One of the princes[21] is this huge, strong guy. Even his name means 'giant'. You find him very aggressive, often angry and sometimes unforgiving. Now Mars rules Aries, whose symbol is the ram. And you know what the term 'rammed' means!"

"Interesting!" said Aliyah. "I guess this prince is symbolic of controlling our energies. How to deal with anger and aggression, how to forgive, even turn the other cheek. That represents a major test of soul progress."

"That's what I think too. Now, the forefinger is ruled by Jupiter. Jupiter also rules Sagittarius, whose symbol is the archer. And what do you know, another prince is a master archer! [22]"

"What's archery got to do with life?" asked Eloise.

---

[21] Prince Bhima
[22] Prince Arjuna

"According to the ancients, the Jupiter finger is the finger of faith," replied Aliyah. "Even the name, Jupiter, comes from Zeus Pater, or Dyaus Pita, implying God the Father."

"But how is that connected with *archery*?"

"Well, faith is that quality within us which helps us reach our goals in life. Hit our target, so to speak. I don't mean faith in God per se, but at least faith in ourselves. It's not by accident that we use the forefinger to point at things. The action and use of faith is like the archer and his arrow."

"Interestingly, it is to this prince that the Godhead reveals an aspect of itself. So the connection with faith and God is even stronger," added Emma.

"I see!" smiled Aliyah. "The crisis of faith, one way or another, is an important test of the soul. Very few can avoid that test in life. I believe this prince had such an experience?"

"Well yes, he faces an enormous crisis of decision and almost gives up. But support from a godly figure reassures him and sets him back on his path. This incident also gives rise to a whole philosophy of life."[23]

"Okay, I see the connection with God and faith," replied Eloise. "What about the middle finger?"

"The middle finger is the tallest, and the corresponding prince is the eldest of them all," continued Emma. "This finger is ruled by Saturn. Saturn is considered the bringer of retribution, evil and despair; the negative effects of reaping what we sow. Saturn also rhymes with Satan, the so-called tempter, who's supposed function is similar."

"That's a curious association!" exclaimed Eloise.

"The association goes further that you think!" said Aliyah. "Saturn rules Capricorn, whose symbol is the goat, which too is a symbol of Satan or devil. Here is another example of the impersonal versus the personal!"

"Okay, so the middle finger represents evil?"

---

[23] The Gita

"Not quite! It represents tests and lessons relating to doing the right thing, discerning good from evil and being righteous. It also represents the trials of retribution for past actions."

"I see, so is this prince righteous or evil?"

"He[24] is the most righteous person in the story, one who cannot tell a lie and who is extremely just. But he is also weak in some ways, unable to always discern good and evil, and most importantly, act on it. This discernment is an important test in life, the ability to choose and act rightly in a situation."

"He messes up, does he?"

"Well, he is a stickler for righteousness, sometimes going by the letter of the law, rather than its spirit. The events that lead to the war are shown as an outcome of his temptation and his fall. He gambles his kingdom, his brothers and his own freedom away; mistakes he made more than once. We see that he learns his lessons the hard way. His tests are always of choosing between the right and the wrong in a situation, even to the finest shade of distinction. He manages to retain his righteousness and sharpen his judgment through most of it, but he isn't perfect."

"So his life is a trial of his righteousness?"

"Exactly! The events that befall him are all engineered to test him in that area."

"Okay, what about the other princes?"

"I gather that they are twins[25], though not identical twins. One of them is extremely handsome and sensual, and the other is a brilliant and knowledgeable statesman who is also very proud of his knowledge."

"How does that relate to the ring finger and the pinky?"

"The little finger is ruled by Mercury, a bisexual god. The test represented by this finger is that of sexuality, which this handsome prince is said to fail in the end. The ring finger is ruled by the Sun, which represents brilliance. It represents the test of wisdom and knowledge, which the other prince also

---

[24] Prince Yudhishtira
[25] The princes Nakula and Sahadeva

failed because of his pride. This finger also represents the test of love, that is, the ability to distinguish love from the sexuality represented by the other finger. These are like twins for many people. Note that we wear the wedding band on this finger, a symbol of love."

"Is that why the princes are twins?"

"Well, Mercury rules Gemini, whose sign is the twins. Now, keep all the fingers of your palm straight and then bend the little finger. You will see that the ring finger also bends! The two are coupled, or couplets, like twins!"

"Yes, they represent the lessons and tests of love," added Aliyah, "usually through separation and heartbreaks, which must come. That's how many of us learn to love through the heart alone, as distinct from physical infatuation. The coupling indicates that we still have some way to go in clearly distinguishing them."

This wasn't much to Eloise's liking and she decided to change tracks. "Okay Mom, but don't you think these are just some funny odd coincidences?"

"I doubt it, for there is even more!" replied Emma. "The war is also a struggle for control of the throne, in the capital city where they live. And the name of this city [26] is derived from a common word that means 'hand'. Too many co-incidences, if you ask me!"

"Alright, then. But what about the enemy in the story? Do they have symbolic meanings too?"

"Yes!" replied Emma. "Their enemies are numerous. Many of those names have meanings like, 'difficult to conquer in battle', 'difficult to subdue', 'one with a bad countenance', ' one who sees evil' and so on.[27] Those names directly point to various natures and sentiments within us. They are not all of a bad kind, only when applied wrongly."

"I see, so the battle is within!"

---

[26] See 'Hasthinapura' in glossary
[27] Duryodhana, Dushasana, Durmukha, Durdharsha etc.

"Curious!" added Aliyah. "That's why both sides are depicted as members of the same family. They are symbolic of natures within us, and therefore they *are* family!"

"The battlefields of life, eh?" Eloise laughed.

"Yes!" agreed Emma. "The story goes on to say that the princes fail in some test or other and are forced to enter hell before entering paradise. In paradise they find that their enemies, the so-called dark seeds, have been transmuted through all their trials, and are also with them! So you see, the story indicates that the trial, tribulation and transmutation of our natures is the purpose behind the battlefields of life!"

"I see. So there *is* something higher to be found in a story of war!" agreed Eloise. "You think such a scripture can also accelerate evil within us?"

"Most scriptures are written in such a way that you could find support for what you want to see!" replied Aliyah. "In this case, you could use it as an excuse to support war on your kin, or believe that death in battle is a ticket to heaven, or even that religion is all nonsense."

"I see, so I have to be careful in reading them!"

"Yes," agreed Aliyah. "But reading and following them is a good way of getting to know ourselves better, and for progressing along our chosen paths. Even the scriptures we are attracted to are a reflection of our choices."

"How would I progress, Mom?"

"Simply watch what all rises up within you, and also in those around you who are following the scriptures. Then choose an interpretation and action based on the fruit it produces, whether it moves you towards greater unity or towards greater separation. Remember that the movement of unity is towards the Godhead, and that of separation, away from it. The scriptures will then take you along the path of your choice."

"You seemed to have ignored her real question of why war exists in a spiritual universe," Emma commented as soon as Eloise had wandered off into the distance.

"I know. She isn't quite the age where she can comprehend, or even needs to," replied Aliyah, gazing thoughtfully after her daughter.

"I must say I find it difficult as well. What do you have to say about it? There is so much meaningless suffering in war."

"Yes, it's perplexing. But war can be seen as a natural outcome of spiritual evolution, much as aggression and killing are part of physical evolution.[28] I should say the use of *force*, rather than war. The less evolved a spiritual species, the more the use of force becomes war-like."

"Still, is it justified at all?"

"From an individual's perspective, it isn't, for sure. In fact, death itself is viewed with so much emotion that it isn't easy to see it objectively."

"Well, that sounds a little heartless to me, to view death without emotion," replied Emma, looking at the rows of crosses in the distance.

"That's precisely the point. The need for that emotional turbulence within us is partly one reason for the apparent illusion of death. Didn't we discuss the role of emotion in our evolution before?[29] Death is one of the means through which our emotions are, what shall I say, plumbed?"

"But death happens anyway, naturally. It is unavoidable, isn't it?"

"I guess you could argue that point. The body can, and does, replace all of its cells every so many years. There is a process of rejuvenation at work. Yet we die, because our cells are programmed to die."

"You mean death is kind of programmed into us?"

---

[28] See chapter 'Path'
[29] See chapter 'Mountain'

"More or less. It's not old age that kills the body. There is a kind of cellular programming that results in their death and thus we get our old-age symptoms."

"This is news to me!" exclaimed Emma.

"But isn't it interesting? The soul does not die as such. The body also need not, but somehow it is forced to die. Do you think it hints that death offers some benefits?"

"Like the emotional experience you mentioned?"

"That is one, yes. Also, without death, there is no evolution.[30] But the fact that a person can be killed has some advantages too, don't you think?"

"I can't think of any, really! That even sounds preposterous!"

"Look at it this way. We tend to build up emotional energy within us, like anger, hatred and so on. This is part and parcel of our evolutionary journey. Now suppose that you have built up an intense hatred for another person, so much so that there is a compulsion to annihilate the other. But if the other person is perceived as immortal, it would be very difficult for you to release that energy, wouldn't it?"

"I guess so."

"If you do not release it in some way, such as through forgiveness, that energy will remain within and become a serious obstacle to your progress. But forgiveness and acceptance are so difficult to come by in the current phase of our evolution. Therefore death and war offers a way for the immortal to achieve the illusion of mortality, and help cleanse some of those energies. There is a tremendous amount of negative emotional energy on our collective shoulders, which is often released through war."

"You can't be endorsing murder!"

"Not at all! There is always the law of retribution, of sowing and reaping, which one cannot escape. You know that. But bottling up those energies can be even more dangerous. They must be released."

---

[30] See chapter 'Tree of Knowledge'

"But then wouldn't that mean an endless cycle? Those who kill will be killed by someone else and so on, ad infinitum? And hatred between souls will never end."

"But there's more than one way to meet the retribution of taking another life!" replied Aliyah. "And one is by *giving* life!"

"Oh? But I have to be a miracle worker for that!"

"You can do it too!" smiled Aliyah. "Can you think of a common episode in life where a human life is *given* to a soul, through a circumstance of pain and blood?"

Emma thought for a moment. "You mean childbirth?"

"Yes! Childbirth and rearing is one way to compensate for it. Murder and hatred need not go on endlessly. In this case, the emotion of hatred can be turned around into one of love, if you notice. The endless cycle you mentioned ceases here."

"I see, so you are saying that birth and death serves some greater purpose?"

"Yes, there are many if you look. But unless and until our emotional nature attains its evolutionary goal[31], death and war must exist."

"But it is still hard to think of death and war as having any positive side."

"True. It must remain fully negative, if it is to make the required impact. But there is more to war than meets the eye. If we step out of our own individuality for a moment and take on a group perspective, we might find more interesting viewpoints."

"Group perspective? What goup perspective?"

"I mean, if you consider humanity or its subgroups as a whole, which have been evolving over the eons, and not just considering an individual or an event at a point in time."

"I see; you are pointing to collective evolution over time. But how can a group perspective on war be any different?"

"Good question. Actually, we give too much credence to individuality. The group is not any less important or less consequential than the individual."

---

[31] See chapter 'Mountain'

"Hmm… you think so?"

"Yes. From a higher viewpoint, one could argue that it is not an individual that's the prime entity, but the group. Even physical evolution rarely bothers about individuals, but works on a species as such.[32] It is of course select individuals that give rise to major changes in the species. The same is true in spiritual group evolution."

"You mean the group evolves at the expense of individuals?"

"If you are talking about bodies, yes, you might say that. It's in more recent times that individuality has become much more significant. During earlier phases, people identified themselves more with the group they were in. Look into history and see all the wars and conflict in the name of kings, nations and ideals."

"But individuality is a good thing, isn't it?"

"Of course! In fact our life-stream has been fragmenting and reinforcing individuality in each of its members. This is a process of expression and exploration. After this, the reverse process can set in, where the individual joins back into the group, bringing in its unique experiences. It's part of returning to the Godhead."

"You mean… lose individuality?"

"Not quite! It's much the same that we see in the history of nations. They come to life, fragment, and create more nations. But then later in their evolution, they start knitting together, forming unions and even merging into larger nations. The present information age is another example, where we see a social, cultural and economic knitting together of nations. Yet each nation or state maintains its identity. It's not a loss of identity, but a curious blend of individuality and cohesiveness into a group."

"Okay, but how does war fit into this?"

"Well, war can also be viewed as a manifestation of the stages of separation within the life-stream. There is a reinforcement of group identities, so that each subgroup or nation can evolve and explore different aspects of being."

---

[32] See chapter 'Tree of Knowledge'

"I see, so the force that creates the separation of groups also fuels war and conflict between them?"

"There is another analogy, if you remember our discussions long ago about thunderclouds.[33] You could think of the cloud as representing a group, and the creation of ice crystals in it representing separation and individuation of sub-groups."

"Yes, I remember that! The crystals rub against each other and create electric charges. These are released as lightning, inside the cloud and also to the outside."

"Ah! You have a good memory! We compared it to war at that time, didn't we?"

"Yeah! I also remember how Thor came into it! That was fun, now looking back!" laughed Emma. "So you seem to be saying that the energies behind war come from the forces of separation?"

"That is one way to look at it. But their effects do not stop there, for they are also forces of selection."

"Now you are really going beyond me. What is this selection?"

"Somewhat like natural selection, if you will. War also selects cultures and modes of life, and also mixes them. It is one of the important ways through which cultures and knowledge were dispersed through nations in the past, creating new cultures and new nations, like progeny. In physical evolution there is the mixing of genes through sexual reproduction and then there is selection from the resulting mix. Something like that also happens here, including a social and cultural mixing and selection."

"You mean war is an evolutionary force?"

"You could say that. It has even some reflection of sexual reproduction, as in physical evolution. Now think of it. There is the violent entry of one nation into another, ravishing and ravaging it. There is blood, destruction of individual cells, and the creation of a new culture that takes characteristics from both parents; isn't this somewhat symbolic of the physical act leading to reproduction?"

---

[33] See chapter 'Storm'

"Whoa! Hey! That's really an oddball viewpoint!"

"Yes it is! But then war is strewn with its symbols. Look at the suggestive shape of its weapons, like swords and catapults, guns and cannons, even missiles and nuclear warheads. But let's drop this line of thinking right here…"

"I agree," Emma snickered.

"I guess I was pointing out that nations are much like species. And there is an evolutionary force at work that develops them, which can exert itself through war. One of those forces is again the law of retribution, of sowing and reaping.[34]"

"You mean the scope of the law goes beyond individuals?"

"Definitely, because an individual is part and parcel of the collective."

"Why do you keep saying that? I make my own decisions. A group doesn't control those."

"But what is an individual, Emma? You are not a single, unitary person as you imagine. You are really a collection of personas. Your so-called identity is really a concept."

"Hey! Hold on a moment! What in the world is a persona? How can I be a concept?"

"Well, the term 'persona' means a kind of social mask we wear, such as the ones we wear to church!" Aliyah smiled. "But a persona is more than a social mask. A lot of our natures are bound up with our various roles, such as wife, mother, friend, patriot, co-worker, boss and so on. Each of these may be called a persona."

"Come again? What are they?"

"They are 'us'! They are aspects of our identity. Each persona is a collection of concepts and feelings."

Emma didn't like the notion at all. "So what binds them together?"

"You could think of a persona as bound together by a unifying concept or feeling, usually related to the roles we play. For example, the concept of motherhood and its nurturing feelings bind together many other associated concepts and natures inside me. This binding creates one of my 'mother' personas. I become that

---

[34] See chapters 'Tree of Knowledge' and 'Chaos'

persona when I talk to Eloise, which is not quite the same one that talks to my husband."

"Yeah!" Emma smiled, "I guess I can relate to that!"

"See, it's not too difficult to think that a lot of what we are, are concepts and natures bound together. Our consciousness is immersed in these collections, somewhat like water in sponge, giving us an identity for the moment."

"Okay, I'll take that with a bit of salt!"

"You may!" smiled Aliyah. "Now a good amount of these natures comes from our cultural and social background. The way we sit, how we talk, the food we eat, things we wear, many of the things that we like or fear; a lot of these are derived from our society and our culture; that is, the collective or the group and its history."

"Okay, but what is your point?"

"My point is this. Not only is our consciousness a fragment of the collective[35], but a lot of concepts and notions that form our identities are also part of the collective. As they change, individual identities also change. We are not as separate as we would like to imagine!"

"Okay, so you are painting a picture of group evolution?"

"Well, you were asking whether the laws of retribution work at the group level. If you see the group as one entity, then you can see some basis for it, no?"

"Maybe," Emma reflected for a moment, "but aren't you also saying that if a nation has set itself on genocide, even those who don't take part are somehow responsible?"

This was a good question and Aliyah considered it a while.

"Yes, I'm somehow reminded of bringing up Eloise! There is a rough analogy, if you like. Now a child may get a spanking on its bottom if it misbehaves. But it doesn't mean that this part of the body or its cells were responsible, does it? Certain concepts within the child expressed through its body and there was retribution."

"That's true."

---

[35] See chapter 'Tree of Life'

"It may be through the hand that some mischief was done, but the pain was administered elsewhere. The consciousness of the child feels it, though other cells in other parts of the body may not. It is when you assign these parts separate identities that all these questions arise."

"But we do have identities, distinct from the group."

"Yes, we have identities that are unique to us, as well as those that are part of the collective. Therefore we are subject to both individual *and* collective retribution."

Emma thought about it.

"From what you say, I seem to be forced to take responsibility for what somebody else does! That doesn't sound right!"

"Yes, but that's from the unique, individual perspective. But if you are really one with humanity, the perspective is different, isn't it?"

"Maybe," Emma again replied thoughtfully. It seemed to make some sense, when she considered the life-stream as a single entity.

Then she had a question, "Is there no escape from the law then? No mercy or forgiveness? It looks like you are painting an even worse picture!"

"On the contrary!" replied Aliyah. "The mechanism we talked about is precisely how forgiveness of sins comes about."

"Why do you say that?" Emma was confused.

"See Emma, any group is part of a larger group, which is part of an even larger group and so on. You could extend it till you encompass the whole of the manifested Godhead."

"Okay, but how does that explain forgiveness?"

"Well, we can adapt the example of the body, where one portion of it received a thrashing. Now think of the manifestations of the Godhead as if it were a single body. It is possible to have retribution fall on a higher and larger entity of much greater grandeur, where the consequences would be of much less significance."

"I see! Then it would look like sins were forgiven. Well then, why doesn't it happen more often? That could avoid a lot of unnecessary suffering for people."

"Not that it couldn't. But let's continue the example of the child again. As the child grows, isn't it given more and more responsibility for its actions? The same is true here too. We are at a stage where our life-stream must learn to meet all the consequences of its actions. That is a very essential part of growing up. Bailouts do happen, individually and collectively, but only to the extent they help us make progress."

"Okay, I get it," replied Emma slowly. "Still, I must say the whole process results in so much evil. Doesn't it?"

"You could say that we are meeting ourselves, and also evolving. What we call as *evil* is a manifestation of the force of fragmentation or separation. It is this force that creates various identities within the Godhead. It is partly because of this that we can see what we are really composed of, what our natures and tendencies are."

"I see, and *good* is also the result of some force?"

"Yes, the force of cohesion and unity, especially love, binds all fragments together, and ultimately causes a return to the original unity of the Godhead. This movement is what we call *good*. Since it is a movement towards the Godhead, you could say that God is good, God is love and so on."

Silence ensued as they watched Eloise walk up to the chapel and enter through the doorway. Lighted candles flickered inside. More people were now seen heading for the chapel.

"It's time for the service," said Aliyah, slowly getting up from the grass. Emma followed. Together they walked towards the chapel.

Aliyah turned back once to gaze at the sky, which was now turning red. Unbeknownst to her, the great synthesis of light and dark within[36] was nearing completion. Soon it would be time to reach beyond duality.

---

[36] See chapter 'Mountain'

17. Exodus

Aliyah, the parting of the red sea, and the grand unification.

"Aliyah, it is time to graduate," whispered the still, small voice within. She recognized the voice and its implication with great excitement. A graduation it was meant to be, indeed, for she had come to recognize the glimmerings of a great plan for the race while engrossed in the mundane activities of bringing up her own daughter. From the almost unconscious beginnings of the baby trying to discover and master its *physical* body, to the *emotional* tantrums of the toddler, to the *mental* development of the primary and the high school kid, and on to college and graduation, she had seen a steady progression which reflected a soul's primordial beginnings, its progressive exploration of physical, emotional and mental realms, through the orderly and planned regimen of learning that was imposed on it, to its graduation from that disciplined learning system.

For the developing child returned again and again to school every year, each time learning new topics and delving deeper into ones already learnt. It had assignments, quizzes and evaluations that decided whether it could move on to the next level. And it was subject to disciplinary actions that in some lands included physical pain for violation of laws. The child often felt constrained in its circumstances, having limited free will to do what it pleased, most of the time being under the watchful eyes of teachers and guardians who prescribed its activities. Here was a perfect reflection of a personality developing through earthly experiences, under the eyes of its soul guides and guardians, and subject to the backlash of the laws of retribution. The personality often wondered about the purpose of the apparently meaningless toil and its inability to control circumstances, and often thought of escape from what it was expected to do by the system.

The child did receive a respite in the form of vacations every year, but only to return soon and continue. Despite the rigorous and apparently monotonous regimen of learning, the child was given ample time for extra-curricular activities, to have fun, and to indulge as it pleased, subject to certain limits. The more mature it got, the greater the freedom it enjoyed. Its greatest freedom came upon graduation, when it was finally free from schooling, and also from the watchful eyes of its teachers and guardians. Aliyah had seen her own daughter take all the school books and study material and fling them into the air, shouting, "Mom, I'm free! I've graduated! No more books and no more studies!" And with that, Eloise had thrown them all into the garage, where they lay for those who might one day find them useful.

It happened over the course of two days. Forty hours of progressively increasing trials and temptations. Aliyah felt turbulent, melancholic and sinister emotions rising within, like floodwaters that rose over levees, threatening to swamp and destroy everything they touched. One by one they came, rising within as a trickle at first, slowly picking up strength and a dreadful periodicity. She tried hard to exercise her will, hold these emotions in check, but there was no stopping the rush of the flood tide. Deep called unto deep, and on it came, its waves and its billows washing over her. She closeted herself and moved into prayer, trying to focus her attention on an imagined point of light within, which soon presented itself before her inner vision, glowing faintly.

As she watched, the fire within suddenly blazed forth, and in that light Aliyah saw herself as she really was for the very first time - not one unitary person that she experienced herself to be, but a multitude of personas[37], changing from one to another, each carrying its own emotions, concerns, memories, fears, and aspirations. And they were all slaving under the tyrannical rule of the mind, *the builder*[38], working day and night, constructing, maintaining and beautifying the various edifices of her life. These personas were now struggling to break free, in a flood tide of emotions. But the mind refused to let go, holding on even tighter to its personas, or what it considered its sole means of survival.

---

[37] See chapter 'War'
[38] The pharaoh in the Exodus story

Shadows now stirred within the depths of her unconscious emotional waters. From there they rose up into her waking consciousness where the waters met the land. Streaks of darkness snaked out from them, ravaging everything they touched, threatening to destroy all that she had built up through the ages. Like plagues, they ravaged the mind, those repressed elementals within her lower self finally set loose after eons of bondage. The shadows rose up high into the air of the mind, and even higher into the sky, blotting out her spiritual sun in a horrifying dark night of the soul.[39] Then the violent tumult within rose to a screaming crescendo and ended quite abruptly with the death of the ego, the firstborn of the mind.[40] The senses, the mind and emotions declutched themselves and she no longer identified with them. The red sea[41] parted, revealing its depths, and the personas streamed out unfettered, carrying with them remembrances of old incidents, forgotten dreams, cravings, fascinations, fears, and also concepts and imaginations utterly strange and foreign.[42] Emotion followed emotion, concepts followed concepts, entities of thought complexes followed others, out from her subconscious and the deep unconscious.

For hours, the exodus continued. Driven by inner guidance, Aliyah managed to isolate herself during most of this time. The multitude of personas that composed Aliyah found little to sustain their natures in that isolation, for the fire had led them into a veritable desert where their tendencies could only burn out. And she trudged on towards a promised land of milk and honey.

But Aliyah never entered the promised land.[43] The neural rewiring process within the brain was consummated and her graduation was now complete. There was no longer any need

---

[39] The plagues move from water, to land, to air and then to the sky, progressing through the elements

[40] The final plague

[41] See chapter 'Sea'

[42] The Israelites carried all sorts of things from the land, during their exodus

[43] Neither did Moses, who was taken (buried) by God

for the books, study material and other paraphernalia. In a quick flash the structure that formed the subconscious and the unconscious emptied out the last of its contents, and Aliyah ceased to exist.

In that emptying was revealed the Light of a thousand suns.

"What do you mean Aliyah is gone?" Theo asked incredulously. "You are right here talking to me."

"Oh, Theo! Aliyah, the individual that you knew, no longer exists! In here there is no personality left. There is only love, intelligence and life!"

At first, Theo was shocked. Had Aliyah gone mad? But she appeared quite normal, in fact pleasant, happy, even nonchalant. Her face was very bright, her eyes twinkling and her very countenance was filled with love. His fears quickly dissipated, and he questioned from a rising curiosity.

"Honey, I don't understand! What has happened to you?"

"Theo, it is nothing miraculous, as you would say. This is as much a physical phenomenon as it is spiritual."

"Don't give me that spiritual mumbo jumbo. Are you going mad? I know you've been going through some hard times."

Aliyah laughed, "Let me explain in terms you will understand. You require a proper reasoning for everything, don't you?!"

"Well, try me! See if you can explain this in a way that makes sense"

"Hmm... What could be more logical than the grand unification?"

"What do you mean the grand unification? You mean like in physics? How is it even related?"

"Theo, both the spiritual and the scientific notions of grand unification are indeed related. It is not difficult to understand the relationship. You know that fundamental science describes everything in terms of principles and energy?"

"Explain that, please."

"Well, everything that exists, every process that happens, occurs through the working of principles and energy. Principles like the law of gravitation, for example, or those of Newton, or Einstein. Even matter is an expression of principles and energy. But a vital ingredient is missing there, which is consciousness."

"Oh no! Consciousness is a product of evolution. It is not fundamental."

"It is both! You see, Theo, your analysis cannot explain the simplest sensations experienced by life forms on the earth. The nature and origin of sensations and feelings, the very experience of pain, pleasure, sight, hearing and others are still a complete mystery. A machine or computer might process signals, but the experience of those signals as sight or hearing is something which it simply would not have. Consciousness is indeed a vital ingredient."

"And how do you propose that organisms acquire this consciousness?"

"Can you take a hypothesis? Let's say the body organizes the fine elements of consciousness latent in matter, and pulls them together into higher amalgamated forms of consciousness, in various life forms. It is then this bodily organization, particularly in the brain, that results in more and more intense feelings and sensations in the higher life forms. Doesn't that make sense?"

"Perhaps," replied Theo, his brows furrowed. "You are saying that consciousness has to be a fundamental property for this to happen. I find that hard to accept. You cannot prove or disprove it, and therefore it has no scientific value."

"Even if you do not agree, let's continue to take it as a hypothesis and see where it takes us. Now if you include this dimension of consciousness, you will see that it is this triad of principles, energy and consciousness that manifest everything, not just principles and energy alone."

"Honey, I fail to see how that has any relevance in our discussion."

"But it has! You see, all the principles and energies that we study derive from a single unified principle and energy, which subdivided into a multitude of principles and energies or forces, finally giving rise to the cosmos as we see it today. This is well known to scientists, and that level of energy at which all principles and forces become one is even called the grand unification energy. But try including this missing dimension of consciousness."

"You are pointing to a unitary trio of principle, energy and consciousness from which everything is derived? Why bring in consciousness when it is not needed for an explanation? It sounds like a creationist version of describing God."

"But you know what? This truth of the grand unification is ancient, known well before fundamental science even started exploring its own versions."

"Honey, you are speaking in riddles. I don't understand you."

"You see, dear, we are discussing principles, energy and consciousness. Principles are but *Truth*. Higher energies when they flow are experienced as *Bliss*. And then there is *Consciousness*. The Aliyah that you see is an expression of this trio. And so are you, though you are not aware of it. Do you know what this unitary triad of *Truth-Consciousness-Bliss* (44) stands for?"

Theo's eyes widened at the realization, for the term she mentioned was familiar to him from ancient religious lore, referring to the Godhead. And he had never expected it to emerge from a discussion of science.

"You mean…?" his voice trailed off as he tried to fully grasp the implication of what she had said. Were these two grand unification concepts similar, perhaps even the same?

"Yes! Now you understand!" She smiled, her eyes twinkling.

Theo was silent for a long time. And then he spoke hesitantly, "So…this is it, then? The end of your journey?"

"The end? Oh no, this is not the end! This is but another beginning!"

Her laughter was like tinkling bells.

Epilogue

Our Father which art in Heaven,
Hallowed be Thy Name.
Thy Kingdom Come.
Thy Will Be Done.
As in Heaven, So in Earth.

Luke 11:2
(KJV)

Glossary

Antipode: The point diametrically opposite to a given point on the surface of the earth (on the opposite side of the earth, so to speak)

Artificial life (or alife): Study of biological systems and processes (like evolution), usually using computers. Artificial life tries to simulate life processes, often from fundamentals, using computer software and/or hardware.

Basho: A renowned Japanese haiku poet. See also Haiku.

Cambrian: A geological period that began nearly 550 million years ago and lasted about 50 million years. During this period there was a tremendous outpouring or 'explosion' of new species on the earth. Pre-Cambrian refers to time periods prior to this Cambrian 'explosion'.

Carbohydrate: The most abundant form of bio-molecules, built from carbon, hydrogen and oxygen (hydrate = add water). Usually found as sugars and starch. A simple form of carbohydrate, called glucose, is the most common energy source used in living cells.

Celestial equator : The projection of the earth's equator out into space, onto the apparent celestial 'sphere' that surrounds the solar system. Since the earth's axis is tilted, this celestial equator is also tilted away from the earth's orbital plane.

Cenozoic (Era): The period after the demise of the dinosaurs (see Mesozoic), till today. Literally, the era of "new life". The Cenozoic Era began roughly 65 million years ago.

Cephalothorax (of spider): The first of the two main parts of the spider. Combines the head and chest area and carries the brain, mouth parts, fangs and the four pairs of legs.

Chakras: Eastern term for energy centers co-located along the spine, with seven major and innumerable minor centers. Chakras other than the root chakra (see also kundalini) are bridges or connections with the higher self.

Christ: The Love facet of the Godhead.

Condensation nuclei (clouds): Water vapor condenses and forms small droplets, even ice, around tiny particles of dust. The dust in this case becomes the nucleus or central portion of the droplet or ice crystal. Smoke, sea salt as well as many air pollutants can also serve as condensation nuclei.

Cones (eye): Photoreceptor cells in the retina of the eye, numbering in a few millions. Cone cells enable the perception of color.

Cross-over (genetic): A biological process that results in the exchange of genes between chromosomes during cell division. One of the sources of genetic variation, making newly formed cells different from one another.

Crust (of the earth): The earth's hard outer layer or shell, which composes the land masses and the sea floor. The crust is distinguished as continental crust and oceanic crust.

Cumulonimbus (cloud): A very tall, dense and menacing thunder cloud, usually with an anvil shape on top and consisting of ice crystals, reaching up to the tropopause (see glossary).

Darwinian evolution/selection: Evolution through natural selection as proposed by Charles Darwin (see evolution). In Darwinian evolution (as opposed to that of Lamarck), acquired characteristics are not inheritable.

Ecosystem: A community of plants, animals and other organisms that interact and coexist within an environment.

Ecliptic: The apparent path of the sun through the "disc" of the zodiac (see glossary), making a great circle through all the constellations.

Embryogenesis: The process by which an embryo within an egg develops into a creature, acquiring form, function and 'life'. Embryogenesis remains largely a mystery, though it is well observed and some of its underlying principles are understood. It is arguably the most complex (and also the most common) process that happens on the planet.

Enlightenment: Literally, 'to be lighted up'. A highly loaded mystical concept, found in various religious and metaphysical contexts. Briefly, it implies the liberation of the personal or lower self.

Equinox: The two intersection points of the great celestial 'circles', viz. the ecliptic and the celestial equator (see glossary). When the earth reaches an equinox point, the center of the Sun is directly over the earth's equator. The two equinox points are called the vernal and autumnal equinoxes, respectively.

Equinox precession: The earth's axis slowly 'wobbles' as it rotates, similar to a spinning top. Consequently, the celestial equator (see glossary) also 'wobbles'. This causes the equinox points to move against the backdrop of the zodiac. The period of one 'wobble' is about 25,765 years, wherein an equinox traverses the twelve zodiac signs. This means that approximately every 2147 years, an equinox enters a different zodiac sign.

Evolution: Loosely, changes in the attributes or traits of an organism or a population over generational time. Usually equated with the principle of 'evolution through natural selection'. Evolution does not imply that populations become any "better" in human terms, only that they become better adapted to do what they do.

Flowering (Induction): Flowering differentiates a mature tree or plant from a juvenile one. Biochemical induction to flowering is thought to be the action of a class of plant hormones called cytokinins, produced in leaves.

Fractals: A mathematical concept of 'fractional dimension' that applies to geometric shapes (other than common geometric figures) that are self-similar. A good example is an idealized fern, the leaves of which resemble another fern each, the leaves of which resemble another fern each, and so on. If the smaller units of such an object look similar to the object itself, then there is self similarity and the object may be loosely described as having a 'fractal' nature. Fractal compositions are commonly found in nature.

Gene pool: Simply put, the collection of all unique genes in a population. All the genes in the pool may not be expressed at a given time, as some may be remaining dormant (unexpressed) in the population.

Haiku: A type of Japanese poetry that uses a few, apparently simple lines to "paint a picture" in the reader's mind.

Hasthinapura: The capital city in the Indian epic of the Mahabharata; the residence of the main players of the story. The name is usually considered a derivation of *Hasthin* (elephant) and *Pura* (city) implying: City of the Elephant(s). The name also allows a more interesting derivation: *Hasth* (hand/palm), *ina* (pertaining to), *Pura* (city). Translated: *The city of the hand.*

Hydrocarbons: Complex chemical compounds built from hydrogen and carbon. Most natural fuels like coal, petroleum and natural gas are composed of hydrocarbons. Hydrocarbons have high energy potential which is released when oxidized (burnt).

Hypsography: Studies the height and depth of various land and sea floor masses against the sea level. Hypsographic charts reveal land and sea mass distribution, and their inter-relationships, if any.

Ionosphere: An atmospheric layer that stretches from 50 miles to nearly 120 miles high, with temperatures exceeding 2500 degrees Fahrenheit under certain conditions. This layer is ionized (molecules split apart into charged ions) by solar radiation. Also known as the thermosphere due to the extreme temperatures in this layer.

Koan: A statement or question that appears nonsensical to the rational mind, but might be understood intuitively. A popular example is "listen to the sound of one-hand clapping".

Kundalini: Literally, 'dweller below'. Sanskrit *'kunda'* means pit or depths and *'lina'* means latent or merged in (there are other meanings as well, but this one is a perfect match). The term refers to energy that is tapped from the earth and distributed into the body by a 'root chakra' which is co-located at the bottom of the spine. The earth being an immense source of energy in human terms, so is the kundalini. This energy is considered feminine. See also 'chakras'.

Mesozoic (Era): The time of the dinosaurs, consisting of the Triassic, Jurassic and Cretaceous periods. Started about 250 million years ago and lasted some 180 million years.

Metabolism: The bio-chemical reactions occurring in cells that help sustain life.

Mountain building: Mountains are thought to be formed as a result of the earth's tectonic plates (see glossary) pressing against one another, causing the crust to rise and fold. The altitude of various land masses are also an effect from the expansion of rock due to heat from below.

Mitosis: The process of cell division whereby a cell divides into two daughter cells, each having identical genetic information as the original cell.

Mutation: A change in the DNA sequence of a gene that potentially changes gene behavior. Mutations are thought to occur randomly, such as due to radiation. Mutations create diversity in the gene pool (see glossary).

Natural selection: In simple terms, the survival of the fittest. Nature 'selects' the genes of those that survive (by killing unfit ones), enabling the survivors to reproduce and pass on their genes. Survival and reproductive ability are capabilities usually attributed to genetic factors. The better (fitter) genes reproduce more and the failed ones disappear or stay dormant in the gene pool.

Plankton: Tiny organisms that thrive en masse in the oceans and other waters. Many types of plankton are capable of photosynthesis, using solar energy to synthesize food. Plankton are more or less the equivalent of plants on land, in terms of the food chain and the sustaining of life on earth.

Photic zone (sea): The upper layer of the sea where light penetrates. Up to about 250 feet below the sea level, the waters are lighted enough for photosynthesis. Light does penetrate further to about 700 feet below sea level, but is not sufficiently strong for photosynthesis.

Photosynthesis: Biochemical reactions that take place in plants (leaves) that use light or energy from the sun, combined with water and carbon dioxide from the air to produce food in the form of carbohydrates such as glucose, sucrose and starch.

Plasma state: At higher temperatures (meaning higher energies), the attraction forces that bind electrons with the positive nucleus of its atom are overcome, enabling them to break free of each other. Often referred to as the fourth state of matter, plasma consists of electrically charged particles like protons and electrons, and also particles like neutrons, moving about akin to molecules in a gas. Much of the stellar 'gas' in the cosmos is in this state.

Prana: Eastern religious term (Sanskrit) referring to vital life force or life energy that permeates the universe. The body is considered to take in prana into itself through the breath (air).

Samskara: Eastern religious term (Sanskrit) referring to an ingrained subtle impression in consciousness which might express as one or more personality traits or tendencies.

Sea-floor spreading: See also Subduction. At divergent boundaries of tectonic plates (see glossary), magma comes up from the deep mantle and spreads out on the sea floor. As the plates are divergent (moving apart), the sea floor extends. The other end of the plates may be subject to subduction. This can create a convection 'current' of matter between the mantle and the crust.

Selective pressure: See also 'Natural Selection'. Refers to the 'pressure' or 'tendency' of an environment to force selection of genes that are better suited for it. An aquatic environment, for example, might 'reward' genes that help create webbed feet. Use of antibiotics, for example, might encourage selection of bacteria that are resistant to those antibiotics (since the rest die and the few survivors reproduce and create a new generation that is resistant to the drug).

Simulation: The imitation of something real, usually in a limited way, for study purposes. A computer may 'simulate' star formation and star distribution in galaxies based on theories or hypotheses. A very useful tool for scientists.

Stratosphere: An atmospheric layer above the tropopause (see glossary) stretching up to 30 miles high. Temperature starts rising with altitude in the stratosphere. The ozone layer is found here, which absorbs most of the harmful ultraviolet rays from the sun.

Subduction (Zone): Process of slipping under. When the earth's plates (see glossary) 'collide' with one another, one of the plates can slide underneath the other, into the mantle. This zone is prone to volcanoes and earthquakes. As a plate slides under, matter is recycled into the deep mantle below. Compensating matter comes up from the mantle at divergent boundaries of plates.

Tectonic plates: The earth's crust that forms the land mass and the ocean floor, is broken into a collection of huge 'plates' that float over the denser mantle (deeper in the earth). These 'plates' move about, resulting in continents drifting apart or coming together over millions of years. The plates 'collide' with each other, creating earthquake and volcanic activity.

Temperature inversion: A deviation from the normal progression of temperature with altitude - such as a sudden increase in temperature in place of an expected decrease, or vice versa.

Tropopause: An atmospheric layer at about 6 miles high where temperature stops decreasing with altitude and starts increasing (see temperature inversion). The tops of thunderclouds usually hit the tropopause and spread out to form an anvil shape.

Truth-Consciousness-Bliss: Eastern mystical conception of the ultimate reality. A literal translation of sat-chit-ananda (Sanskrit). Considered one of the highest experiences of oneness on the theistic path.

Vasana: Eastern religious term (Sanskrit) for a congenital personality trait, the expression of a samskara (see glossary).

Zodiac: Ancient term used for constellations in the sky. The orbits of the various planets form something of a disc around the sun, and the stars in the sky viewed along the periphery of this disc are divided into twelve 'constellations' or zodiac signs, commonly found in astrological treatises. Each zodiac constellation is given a symbol (usually an animal) and a name.

PHOTO/IMAGE CREDITS

Woman Archer: Dominique Douieb, PhotoAlto.com
Cyclone Catarina: NASA image in Public Domain
Earth image: NASA image in Public Domain
Sun with rainbow-like arch: Vedic Design (www.vedicdesign.com)
Big Cumulonimbus cloud: Image from Flickr.com, User: Nicholas_T,
    Creative Commons Attribution 2.0 Generic License
Astronomical Clock: Image by Judith from Flickr.com, User: judepics,
    Creative Commons Attribution 2.0 Generic License
Leaf-cutter ant: Wikimedia Commons, Scott Bauer, US Department of
    Agriculture, Creative Commons Attribution 2.5 license
Spider in Chapter 'Web': Wikimedia Commons, User:Shyamal,
    Creative Commons Attribution 2.5 license
Sooty tern (Sterna Fuscata) Egg: Forest & Kim Starr, United States Geological
    Survey, Creative Commons Attribution 3.0 United States License
Sepia Sea Scape: Image by "Dom H UK/Dom Hine", Flickr.com,
    Creative Commons Attribution 2.0 Generic License
Road to Twyfelfontein: Image by "SqueakyMarmot/Mike", Flickr.com,
    Creative Commons Attribution 2.0 Generic License
Confederate Angel: Image by "DWQ/David W Quinn", Flickr.com,
    Creative Commons Attribution 2.0 Generic license
Wings of Grace: Image by "métrogirl", Flickr.com, Creative Commons
    Attribution 2.0 Generic license
Cosmic Microwave Background radiation map: NASA/WMAP Science Team
Lightning bolts: NOAA (National Oceanic and Atmospheric Administration/
    Department of Commerce)

Other royalty-free images acquired from Fotolia.com and BigStockPhoto.com
(2007/2008). Their copyright holders, in no particular order:

Andrea Hornackova (US), Edward White(Ireland), Eric Gevaert(Netherlands),
Darko Novakovic (Serbia/Montenegro), Gary/fotolia(USA), José
Elias(Portugal), Ekaterina Fedorova (Russia), objectsforall/fotolia(Estonia),
Valua Vitaly (Ukraine), Marzanna Syncerz (Poland) ,Cynthia Inhoff (USA),
Barry Sherbeck (USA), Manuel Fernandes(Portugal), James Steidl (USA),
AlienCat/fotolia(USA), Clara Natoli (Norway), Goce Risteski
(Serbia/Montenegro), Georgios Kollidas (Greece), Rohit Seth (Canada),
Alessandro Bolis (Italy), Travis Manley(USA), Eric Gevaert (Netherlands),
Feng Yu (Canada), Chris Harvey (United Kingdom), Cre8tive
Studios/fotolia(Australia), Yuri Trots (Russia), Anika Salsera(Canada),
mkb/fotolia(India), Andres Rodriguez (United Kingdom),
36Clicks/fotolia(Netherlands)

Cover concept: The Archress (Lady Arjuna) by John, Rekesh.
Interior composite images composition by John, Rekesh

CPSIA information can be obtained
at www.ICGtesting.com
Printed in the USA
LVOW08s2320250717
542519LV00001B/109/P